Merch Resources
For
Merch By Amazon
Designers

Message me at m.me/chris
or email chris@merch.co
to get the *digital version* of this book
with **CLICKABLE LINKS** for free!

**Want to
MAKE MONEY
by simply
GIVING THIS BOOK AWAY?**

**Learn how at
MasteringMerch.com**

Merch Resources for Merch By Amazon Designers

Green, Chris

ISBN-13: 978-1546930822
ISBN-10: 1546930825

First Printing: May 2017

DISCLAIMER:

About the author:

Chris Green

Chris Green has spent the last decade working with Amazon as a seller, vendor, and author. He is also seen as an Amazon ambassador or evangelist, encouraging others to find their own success with the different Amazon platforms such as FBA, Merch By Amazon, CreateSpace, Kindle, and more. He enjoys life in Massachusetts with his beautiful wife and two kids.

ChrisGreen.com
chris@chrisgreen.com
214-298-6866 (call or text)
Facebook.com/chris

youtube.com/chrisgreen2
twitter.com/it <-- yes, @it
instagram.com/locomodem

merch.co

snapchat.com/add/locomodem

We are planning a Merch Conference!
Sign up here to get details:
MerchConference.com

What is The RiverBank?

The River stands for Amazon and Bank is for making money. If you're making money on Amazon, then you're on The RiverBank!

We have set up a *first-of-it's-kind* online community focused on Merch By Amazon.

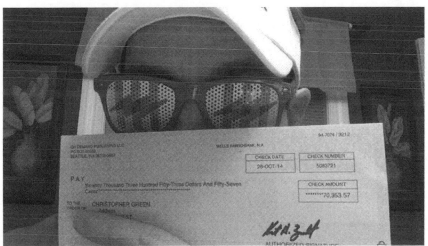

In addition to Merch By Amazon, I also teach about CreateSpace and Kindle publishing. This is my largest MONTHLY ROYALTY CHECK from selling BOOKS!

The RiverBank is built on Facebook Workplace, which is a PAID VERSION of Facebook. That means that it has all of the same functionality, utility, and familiarity of Facebook but with added features and controls. It means no ads, no spam, and better organization and alerts of the content that you've been getting from Facebook.

What else do members of The RiverBank get?

Monthly LIVE webinars (ask questions live or watch replays) with **PAID INDUSTRY EXPERTS**!

Copyright, trademark, and patent lawyers!

Facebook advertisers and marketers!

Adobe Photoshop and Illustrator demonstrations!

These are just some of the knowledgeable contributors to
The RiverBank with more being added!

Facebook Workplace PROFILES

You can see that your RiverBank profile page is very similar to our regular Facebook profile page. You can follow other members, start Messenger chats, post pictures or videos, and even use Facebook Live.

You can upload a profile picture and image of your choice and change them at any time.

Facebook Workplace GROUPS

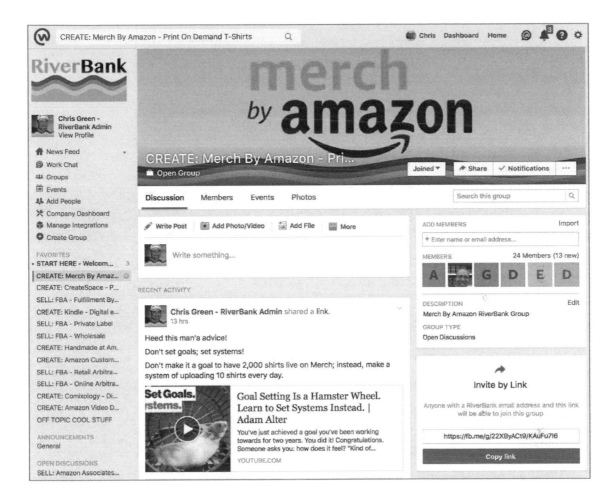

Just like the RiverBank profile pages, the RiverBank newsfeed looks and functions very similar to your regular Facebook newsfeed. You will see updates from your groups and posts from people that you follow.

You also have links on the left side to help you quickly navigate to different parts of the Riverbank Workplace.

Facebook Workplace NEWSFEED

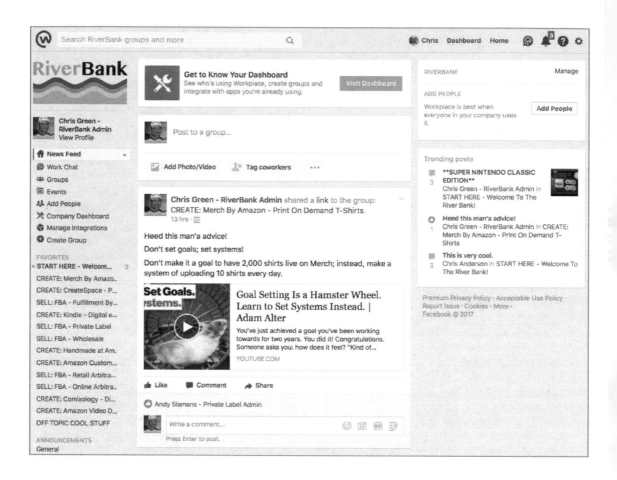

Just like the RiverBank profile pages, the RiverBank newsfeed looks and functions very similar to your regular Facebook newsfeed. You will see updates from your groups and posts from people that you follow.

You also have links on the left side to help you quickly navigate to different parts of the Riverbank Workplace.

The RiverBank Merch By Amazon Facebook group is built on Facebook Workplace It even has dedicated apps (including Workplace Messenger!) that bring all of the same familiar Facebook functionality to this private community!

The RiverBank is $19/month with a 30-day free trial.
Sign up at River-Bank.com

Table of Contents

1 - Merch By Amazon

Merch by Amazon Overview

Merch by Amazon makes it easy for you to create, promote and sell your branded merchandise with no risk and no up-front costs. You simply supply the artwork, choose the t-shirt type and color(s), and then promote your shirts in your app, blog or on social media. Amazon takes care of the rest, including production, sales, shipping and creating a product page on Amazon.com - all at no cost to you.

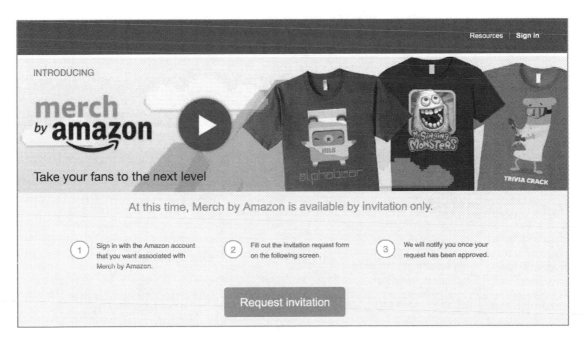

Official Merch By Amazon Links:

Login/request an invitation:
merch.amazon.com

Best Practices:
merch.amazon.com/resource/201849250

Royalty Calculation:
merch.amazon.com/resource/201858580

Content Policy:
merch.amazon.com/resource/201858630

SHIRT TEMPLATE (PSD, AI):
merch.amazon.com/resource/201851710

FAQs:
merch.amazon.com/resource/201846470

LEGAL:
merch.amazon.com/resource/201859880

Report Infringements:
amazon.com/gp/help/reports/infringement

Amazon Developer Forum (Merch):
forums.developer.amazon.com/spaces/80/index.html

To upload an image to Merch By Amazon, it must be a 4500 x 5400 PNG file under 25 MB.

Recommended resolution is 300 DPI although 72 DPI (and everything in between) will also work.

Any other dimensions, file formats, or larger than 25 MB will not work. There are no exceptions.

When working with designers, communicate these requirements to them to avoid potential confusion.

2 - 'Must Read' Blogs

michaelessek.com

About Michael Essek:

Hello! I'm Michael Essek.

I'm a full-time T-Shirt Seller, Illustrator and Designer from the UK.

In the summer of 2013 I began producing designs for T-Shirts, and uploading them to sites like Redbubble & Society6. Shortly after this I began selling through my 'own-brand' t-shirt website.

I have had designs featured on TeeFury, BustedTees, ShirtPunch, and other popular T-Shirt sites.

By the end of the first year my profits from such sites were averaging a minimum of $1000/month. After 3 years my earnings are around $7000/month. This income is almost entirely passive, required very little upfront financial investment, and relies on no paid marketing. I don't print T-Shirts myself and I don't handle stock.

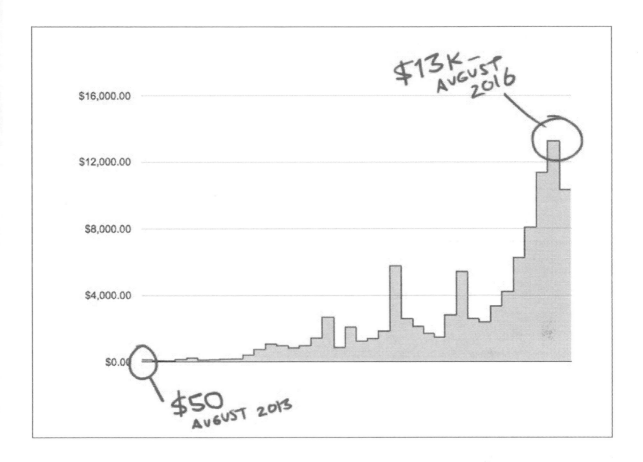

(My T-Shirt earnings since 2013 – as of midway through September 2016. The tall blue line – August 2016 – represents just over $13k in profit).

I believe that anyone with competent design abilities can achieve similar (if not much better) results within a similar timeframe, thanks to the ever-increasing methods for creative individuals to make money online.

All you need is the ability to create designs (or commission them), some good ideas, a willingness to learn, and dedication.

This blog is a place for me to share what I have learned (and continue to learn) about generating and growing passive income from creative work. I believe the advice I share will help you to start making money from your designs – or to increase your earnings if you are already selling your artwork online.

michaelessek.com

Using Print-On-Demand T-Shirt Fulfillment Companies: Advice & Tips For Designers Using Printful, Teelaunch, CustomCat Etc.

Last Updated: May 12, 2017

Are you looking at using a **Print-On-Demand T-Shirt fulfillment company** like Printful, CustomCat or Teelaunch to do the printing and shipping for your clothing brand or business?
If so, I have some advice for you.

I've been using Print-On-Demand T-Shirt Fulfillment companies *(or T-Shirt Dropshippers)* for over 3 years now – and in that time I've dealt with pretty much every issue you could ever expect.

Read more at:
michaelessek.com/print-on-demand-t-shirt-fulfillment-companies

Got Your Merch By Amazon Approval? 4 Strategies To Help You Tier Up Fast

Last Updated: April 27, 2017

When you get your **Merch By Amazon** account approval, you get just 10 design 'slots' to fill.
In order to increase your total number of slots (or 'tier up') – you need to make at least 10 sales.

Note: Amazon actually says that tiering up is not based *solely* on sales. And I quote: "*Admission to these tiers are based not only on sales, but the quality of the products being sold by the content creator as well.*" Worth knowing!

Anyway – as you climb through the tiers you should find it gets easier to make sales, because – *generally speaking* – the more designs you have live, the greater your chances of generating sales.

Read more at:
michaelessek.com/merch-by-amazon-approval-tier-up-fast

10

2017 Q1 Review [Merch By Amazon vs. Redbubble vs. Teepublic] + 3 Big Lessons

Last Updated: April 10, 2017

Yes, the first quarter of 2017 is over already! yikes!

So it's time for a review post.

Hold on to your hats.

Let's Look At Those Numbers!

Read more at:
michaelessek.com/merch-amazon-q1-earnings-review

How To Outsource T-Shirt Designs The Right Way (+ Mistakes To Avoid)

Last Updated: April 10, 2017

With the increasing growth in the Print-On-Demand T-Shirt industry – and platforms like Merch By Amazon – demand has increased for cheap and easy T-Shirt designs.

This has flooded the market with designers offering T-Shirt artwork at very low prices (eg. from $5 per design through sites like Fiverr) – which can appear very tempting for newcomers looking to get a lot of designs for as low a price as possible.

And although what constitutes a 'quality' design is subjective, there are a lot of ways in which cheap designs can be a liability, rather than an asset.

Read more at:
michaelessek.com/outsource-t-shirt-designs-right-way-mistakes-avoid

12

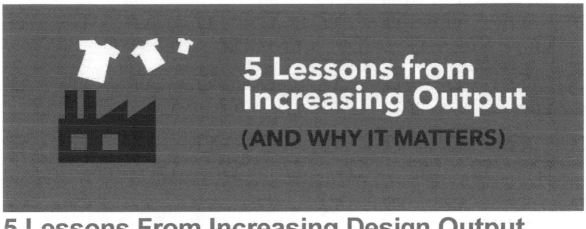

5 Lessons From Increasing Design Output (And Why It Matters)
Last Updated: April 10, 2017

December 2016 was my best month ever for T-Shirt sales and income.
It blew everything up to that point out of the water.

But – if I'm honest – I was somehow a little disappointed, and felt it could have been better.

Why?

Because the total number of design available on my single biggest sales channel (**Merch By Amazon**) was significantly diminished throughout November and December (through a combination of Amazon's introduction of the new 60-day-rule, plus a crackdown on designs that violated Amazon's design policies).

Read more at:
michaelessek.com/increasing-t-shirt-design-output

Selling T-Shirts on Seller Central with Shopify: Part 2 (Overcoming Headaches)
Last Updated: April 10, 2017

Last week we took a look at how to sell T-Shirts on Amazon Seller Central.

If you aren't familiar with **Seller Central** – or the difference between Seller Central and a platform like **Merch By Amazon** – then go back and read last week's blog for a detailed run through.

In short though: Seller Central has some distinct advantages over a platform like Merch – and thanks to the new Shopify integration with Amazon, **we can effectively sell T-Shirts on auto-pilot**.

Read more at:
michaelessek.com/selling-t-shirts-seller-central-shopify-part-2-overcoming-headaches

14

Selling T-Shirts On Amazon Merch vs. Seller Central – Pros & Cons (& Headaches)

Last Updated: April 10, 2017

Update! A lot of the issues discussed in this post have since been resolved, please see this blog post for an updated version.

Let's talk about Amazon!

When it comes to selling T-Shirts on Amazon, you have a couple of options.

1) **Merch By Amazon**. You upload artwork – and Amazon prints and ships the T-Shirts for you – paying you a percentage of each sale made.

2) **Amazon Seller Central**. You sell Shirts *directly* to customers *via* Amazon, and are responsible for the printing and shipping.

Read more at:

michaelessek.com/selling-t-shirts-amazon-merch-vs-seller-central

15

Selling T-Shirts On Instagram: 3 Marketing Tips

Last Updated: April 10, 2017

If you've been reading my blog for anytime at all, then you'll know my main source of income – and what I write about most often – is **selling T-Shirts through print-on-demand platforms like Merch By Amazon and Redbubble**.

Almost all of those sales come *organically*.
That means I don't do much 'direct' marketing of my own, and I do almost no **paid-marketing** (i.e. Advertising).
Well, that is beginning to change.

I've been playing around with Shopify for a few months now, and am beginning to see some success using **paid traffic** via Instagram – specifically by reaching out to popular, relevant accounts and paying them for sponsored posts.

Read more at:
michaelessek.com/selling-t-shirts-on-instagram

16

Brands and Branding while Selling T-Shirts Online: Your Questions Answered

Last Updated: April 10, 2017

When it comes to selling T-Shirt online, branding is one of the things you'll wrestle with sooner or later.

- Should you have *one* T-Shirt 'brand' for all your designs – or **several**?

-

- Should you keep your brand identity *specific* to a single niche, or broad and general to appeal to as many people as possible?

-

- Should you brand yourself as an individual artist / designer, *or* as a business / company?
  These are questions I get asked a lot, so I thought I'd delve into some of the various considerations here…

Read more at:
michaelessek.com/brands-and-branding-while-selling-t-shirts-online-your-questions-answered

2016 Year In Review [$100k Profit, Channel Breakdown and 2017 Plans]

Last Updated: April 10, 2017

2016 is over – so it's time for a review post.

This isn't going to be a particularly long or exhaustive article – more of a brain dump. I just want to share my raw numbers and pull out some major headlines, plus explain my thinking and plans for 2017.

2016 was a big year for me.

Read more at: michaelessek.com/t-shirt-income-review-100k-profit-2016

How To Sell More Shirts!
[Second Edition]

Fully Revised & Updated **Strategies, Tips And Tricks** To Help You **Sell T-Shirts Online** with Merch By Amazon And Print-On-Demand Sites - *Even If You've Never Sold A T-Shirt Before!*

Grow Your Own T-Shirt Business
How To Start, Where To Sell & How To Scale
From Print-On-Demand To *Your Own Brand*

Grow Your Own T-Shirt Business

How To Start, Where To Sell & How To Scale – **From Print-On-Demand To Your Own Brand**

What's Inside:

- How I went from **ZERO** to **$10,000/month** from T-Shirt sales in 3 years

- A **Full Breakdown** and analysis of the various T-Shirt sites you can sell on – and which ones are best for YOUR DESIGNS

- The **5 Biggest Mistakes** that almost all new T-Shirt designers and sellers make, *and how to avoid them*

- *and much, much more!*

Price: **$39.99**

| Full Details | Buy Now: $39.99 |

michaelessek.com/chris

2 Book Bundle Special Offer
Get **How To Sell More Shirts! [Second Edition]** together with **Grow Your Own T-Shirt Business** (plus FREE bonuses!)

Get Both Books [Plus Bonuses] – And Save!

What's Included:

- **How To Sell More Shirts** [Second Edition]

- **Grow Your Own T-Shirt Business**

- **Private Facebook Group** Access

- *(Normal Price: $69.98+)*

Bundle Price: just **$49.99**

| Full Details | Buy Now: $49.99 |

michaelessek.com/chris

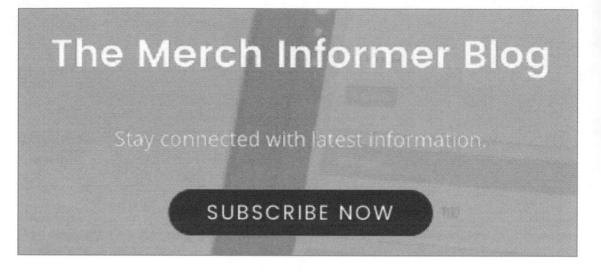

merchinformer.com/blog

The Founders

Neil L:
Internet marketer, growth hacker, and passive income expert featured by Entrepreneur.com and CNBC.com.

Todor K:
Old School Internet Marketer, Merch Early Adopter, Serial Entrepreneur

Merch By Amazon Early Adopters

Both Todor and Neil started on Merch almost as soon as it was opened. Already selling items on Amazon via FBA, they were very familiar with how everything worked and were amazed at the opportunity to sell products on the biggest marketplace in the world without holding inventory. They saw an opportunity and got to work.

Selling via Merch ended up being very lucrative for them. As they ran other internet businesses at the same time, they decided to sell off one of their T-Shirt companies. To their knowledge, this was the first company that utilized Merch and was sold for $73k.

The account that is still held enjoys a nice high four-figure income each and every month. They know exactly what it takes to be successful with Merch by Amazon and created Merch Informer to help other people reach the level of success they have enjoyed with this new platform.

merchinformer.com/blog

How To Use Upwork To Outsource And Scale Your Merch Business May 22, 2017

When you first get accepted to Merch by Amazon, it is one of the best feelings ever! You have 10 slots available with 2 uploads per day. The possibilities seem endless (and they are!). What we recommend is always to dive in headfirst. Get a good feel for the research process, understand how BSR correlates with sales, and then figure your way around a set of design tools. It could be Photoshop; it could be GIMP, or something simple like Make-Merch. No matter what you decide to use, just get to know how to design yourself.

Read more at:
merchinformer.com/use-upwork-outsource-scale-merch-business

<u>Ultimate AMS (Amazon Marketing Services) Guide to Marketing Your Merch</u> May 16, 2017

When Merch by Amazon began, the program was targeted at app developers. Once the news was out about this program that would allow you to sell products on Amazon and produce a royalty without dealing with customers or inventory, people absolutely flooded the Merch by Amazon signup page, and they became invite only.

Since then competition has grown and so have the amount of people selling merch through MBA. Some people say it has gotten harder to sell shirts, some thing it is still easy as ever. The one thing that everyone has been missing though is the ability to run ads to their Merch by Amazon shirts if they were not app developers. There was no option to run cost per click ads to shirts like there is in seller central for people doing FBA.

Read more at:
merchinformer.com/ultimate-ams-amazon-marketing-services-guide-to-marketing-your-merch

Growth Hacking Pinterest To Sell Amazon Merch May 8, 2017

How many times have you seen someone mention or felt that you were just not getting any sales through Merch by Amazon leaving frustrated even though they were all posted on social media? Social media can be one of the biggest opportunities for selling your Merch if you do it correctly. The fact is though, that simply posting your shirts to social media is not going to work unless you put in the legwork first.

Read more at:
merchinformer.com/growth-hacking-pinterest-to-sell-amazon-merch

Merch Pricing Strategies – Why You Are Leaving Money On The Table April 24, 2017

Since we started Merch Informer, we have seen almost every pricing strategy in the book. This is something that most people will probably never agree completely on, and thus, has been the topic of hot debate in the past. Should you price high to be seen as the premium option? You WILL make the most royalty per shirt this way, that is for sure. Should you price right in the middle of the pack of designs and try to compete less on price, but more on unique, amazing designs? Or, do you throw all of that out the window and attempt to make only a few cents per shirt sale and price at the bottom of the barrel in the hopes that you will stick out among the thousands of people you might competing with. "Have some self respect!" some might say.

Read more at:
merchinformer.com/merch-by-amazon-pricing-strategies

Results ⓘ	Reach ⓘ	Cost per Result ⓘ	Amount Spent ⓘ
43,797 Link Clicks	872,659	$0.01 Per Link Click	$520.11
4,543 Link Clicks	65,018	$0.01 Per Link Click	$23.36
551 Link Clicks	4,695	$0.01 Per Link Click	$6.49
16,617 Link Clicks	395,012	$0.01 Per Link Click	$195.71
16,124 Link Clicks	292,356	$0.01 Per Link Click	$162.47
9,049 Link Clicks	175,252	$0.01 Per Link Click	$122.96
969 Link Clicks	18,735	$0.02 Per Link Click	$16.28
201 Link Clicks	3,993	$0.06 Per Link Click	$12.48
91,851 Link Clicks	1,514,221 People	$0.01 Per Link Click	$1,059.86 Total Spent

How To Run Facebook Ads To Merch by Amazon Listings
April 17, 2017

How many of you just landed on this guide and have already tried running paid advertising to your merch listings? Out of all the people that have, I bet the vast majority of you ran paid advertising using Facebook ads and reported back that they were expensive and a waste of time.

Read more at:
merchinformer.com/how-to-run-facebook-ads-to-merch-by-amazon-listings

A Definitive Guide On Seasonal Niches – How To Find, Rank, And Manage Your Listings April 10, 2017

Seasonal niches can be a massive money maker when it comes to listing Merch on Amazon if you know what you are looking for and how best to manage these niches. If I were to say the word "seasonal niche" to you, what is the first thing that would come to mind? For most, it would be the major holidays: Christmas, Thanksgiving, Easter, so on and so forth.

Read more at:

merchinformer.com/amazon-merch-seasonal-niches

Which POD Service Should You Use To Sell On Amazon?
April 3, 2017

We have been receiving a lot of questions lately on which print on demand platform is the best for listing your merchandise on Amazon. Todor and I are huge advocates of mixing all three when building your brand because each has its own benefits (and drawbacks of course). In the article below we are going to cover the advantages of these platforms/integrations and how to best utilize each of them when growing your merchandise business.

Read more at:
merchinformer.com/pod-service-use-sell-amazon

Merch Informer Case Study – A Merch By Amazon 20k Per Month Blueprint March 27, 2017

Todor and I started Merch Informer just around 6 months ago. Ever since the beginning, we have been Merchants ourselves, practicing exactly what we preach on how to find successful designs, dominate markets, and crush the competition. Month in and month out, we are making more profit from Merch by Amazon and the multiple integrations that are now available for Amazon merch sellers.

Read more at: merchinformer.com/case-study-merch-by-amazon-blueprint

Teespring Amazon Integration – Zero Cost Startup Guide
March 19, 2017

One of the biggest industries that the internet has seen has been Merchandise and this sector has been growing by absurd numbers year in and year out. I have never really been someone to buy much in terms of Merch but a little over a year ago, I found myself engrossed in the industry. This spawned myself and business partner clearing hundreds of thousands of dollars and launching Merch Informer. Selling Merch allows you to be creative and also business minded!

Read more at:
merchinformer.com/teespring-amazon-integration-zero-cost-startup-guide

Zero Cost Merch Marketing March 13, 2017

For one reason or another, the majority of Merch by Amazon users are not willing to spend money to actually market the goods they work so hard to create. While this is not recommended (we have lots of guides on how to drive your own traffic), there is nothing wrong with wanting to ride the Amazon gravy train as long as possible.

Read more at:
merchinformer.com/zero-cost-merch-marketing

CURRENTLY IN FREE BETA

Make Merch Blog: http://make-merch.com/blog/

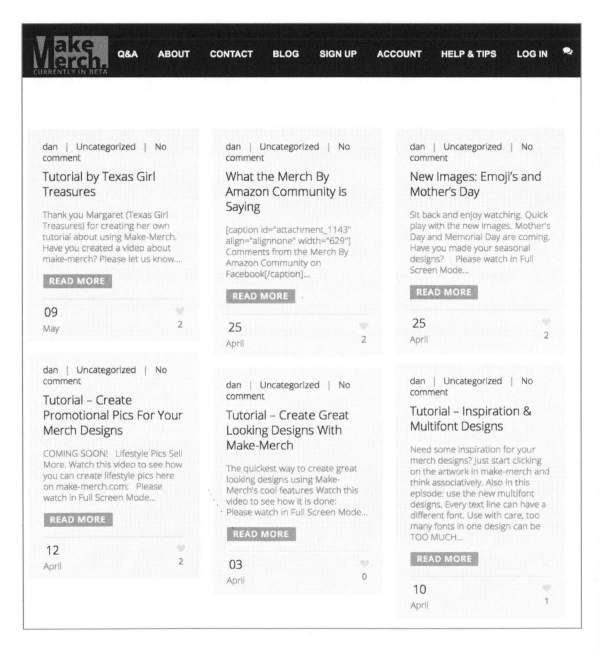

dan | Uncategorized | No comment

Tutorial by Texas Girl Treasures

Thank you Margaret (Texas Girl Treasures) for creating her own tutorial about using Make-Merch. Have you created a video about make-merch? Please let us know...

READ MORE

09
May

2

dan | Uncategorized | No comment

What the Merch By Amazon Community is Saying

[caption id="attachment_1143" align="alignnone" width="629"] Comments from the Merch By Amazon Community on Facebook[/caption]...

READ MORE

25
April

2

dan | Uncategorized | No comment

New Images: Emoji's and Mother's Day

Sit back and enjoy watching. Quick play with the new images. Mother's Day and Memorial Day are coming. Have you made your seasonal designs? Please watch in Full Screen Mode...

READ MORE

25
April

2

dan | Uncategorized | No comment

Tutorial – Create Promotional Pics For Your Merch Designs

COMING SOON! Lifestyle Pics Sell More. Watch this video to see how you can create lifestyle pics here on make-merch.com: Please watch in Full Screen Mode...

READ MORE

12
April

2

dan | Uncategorized | No comment

Tutorial – Create Great Looking Designs With Make-Merch

The quickest way to create great looking designs using Make-Merch's cool features Watch this video to see how it is done: Please watch in Full Screen Mode...

READ MORE

03
April

0

dan | Uncategorized | No comment

Tutorial – Inspiration & Multifont Designs

Need some inspiration for your merch designs? Just start clicking on the artwork in make-merch and think associatively. Also in this episode: use the new multifont designs. Every text line can have a different font. Use with care, too many fonts in one design can be TOO MUCH...

READ MORE

10
April

1

New Images:
Emoji's and Mother's Day

Sit back and enjoy watching. Quick play with the new images. Mother's Day and Memorial Day are coming. Have you made your seasonal designs?

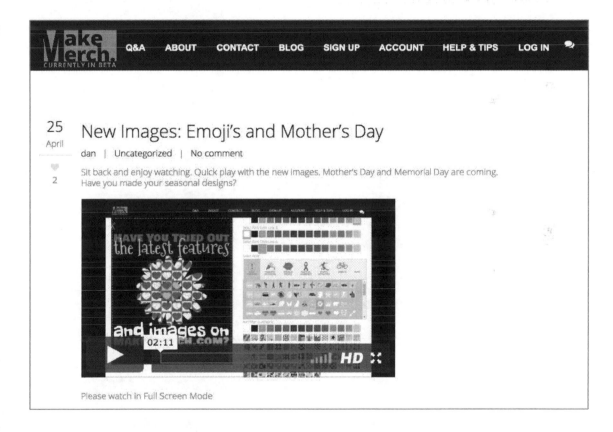

Read more at:
make-merch.com/2017/04/25/new-images-emojis-and-mothers-day

PlaceIt Blog
blog.placeit.net

Placeit Blog

[PERSUASIVE COPY HERE]

How To Create Teespring Facebook Ads Like A Professional

MAY 18, 2017 IN MARKETING

Comprehensive List of Best Tshirt Templates and Generators

MAY 15, 2017 IN DESIGN, MARKETING

How To Create Teespring Facebook Ads Like A Professional

MAY 18, 2017

With an ever growing user base and people increasingly spending more time on Facebook, Facebook is the perfect place to advertise your business. Facebook has successfully turned itself into an advertising medium by connecting advertisers to its massive user base. Many wondered what was Facebook's revenue model since it spent so many years being an ad-free social media platform. And then suddenly, we started seeing ads all over Facebook, Instagram, and Snapchat. Truth is that for advertisers, it's probably the most cost-effective way to advertise a business and get incredible results!

Read more at:
blog.placeit.net/teespring-facebook-ads

How to Make a T-Shirt Design From Scratch
APRIL 21, 2017

A Complete Guide on How to Make a T-shirt Design

If you run a t-shirt business, you know how important it is to find a way to make quality t-shirt designs in as little time as possible to optimize your production process and start earning money ASAP. Sounds expensive and complicated? Not really, making your very own t-shirt design doesn't have to be hard and you don't necessarily have to have graphic design skills to make a killer t-shirt.

There are two paths you can go by for making your own t-shirt design: downloading graphics and fonts and using Photoshop to put them together for a totally DIY t-shirt design or using a t-shirt template from a design generator that lets you get creative while taking care of all the technicalities for you.

I tested both alternatives by making my very own Mother's Day t-shirt design from zero, here's how it went.

Read more at:
blog.placeit.net/how-to-make-a-t-shirt-design

How to Make Great Facebook Ads to Sell More T-Shirts

MARCH 21, 2017

Make Great Facebook Ads to Sell More T-Shirts

First things first, **Facebook reigns**. Is this clear? If not, here's a graph that demonstrates it. By January 2017, Facebook had 1.8 billion monthly active users. In other words, Facebook has 1.8 billion targetable users! This is the main reason why advertising on Facebook makes a lot of sense and if you are still not advertising on Facebook you are definitely missing out.

Read more at:

blog.placeit.net/how-to-make-great-facebook-ads-to-sell-more-t-shirts

3 - Merch Research

MerchInformer.com

Realize Your
Merch Potential

**Amazon Merch research simplified and streamlined putting
more money In your pocket**

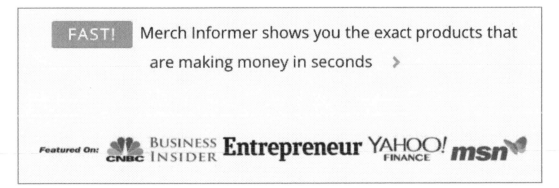

Fully Secure

As merchants ourselves, we understand how important it is to keep data safe and secure. Merch informer does not give away any of the designs that you discover in any hidden database.

Niche Data

Merch Informer gives you all the niche data at your fingertips to help you make decisions. Find out what consumers want and exactly what is selling! Finding high opportunity items based on Amazon sales data has never been easier.

Organized

Finding designs is the easy part. Keeping them organized can sometimes be a real struggle. Say goodbye to all your spreadsheets and say hello to the sleek Merch Informer solution.

Lightning Fast

Merch Informer makes you more money with a fraction of the time invested. Save your time for more important things and let us help you navigate the expanding Amazon Marketplace.

Product Research

The power of niche research comes from looking up keywords on Amazon and seeing exactly what products and designs are selling! Find out what potential customers are buying today without the need to guess what they may like.

Sort and filter between designs and categories in seconds seeing what you need to do in order to sell more. Designed for sellers, get detailed information on:

- Product Brand
- ASIN
- Price (High, Low, Average, Current)
- Features
- Description
- Best Sellers Rank (Main Category)
- Estimated Monthly Sales
- Trademark
- Competition

Now upgraded with our newly released estimated sales numbers based on thousands of data points!

Brand Spy

Quickly examine your competition by looking at what other Merchants/Brands are selling! Choose a product category and pull up their 100 best selling items in seconds. Many of our customers are finding this feature useful to extrapolate how well a brand is doing from releasing products in specific niches.

Not only is the Merchant/Brand search useful for taking a look at others, you can use it track your very own brand. This will allow you to see a snapshot of how your brand is doing and what you could possibly do to improve it.

Keyword Finder/Keyword Favorites

The game has been changed with the release of the new keyword finder!

Amazon is a big data company that knows exactly what products and phrases to recommend to people in order to get them to buy. When customers start typing, Amazon is suggesting products and niches that they know are hot.

With the new keyword finder, simply enter in a seed keyword, and get hundreds of auto suggest Amazon keywords that are proven sellers! Organize your favorite keywords through favorites, check the phrase for trademark, and check their competition with the click of a button.

Using the Merch Informer Keyword Finder is the fastest way to earn more money selling Merch on Amazon!

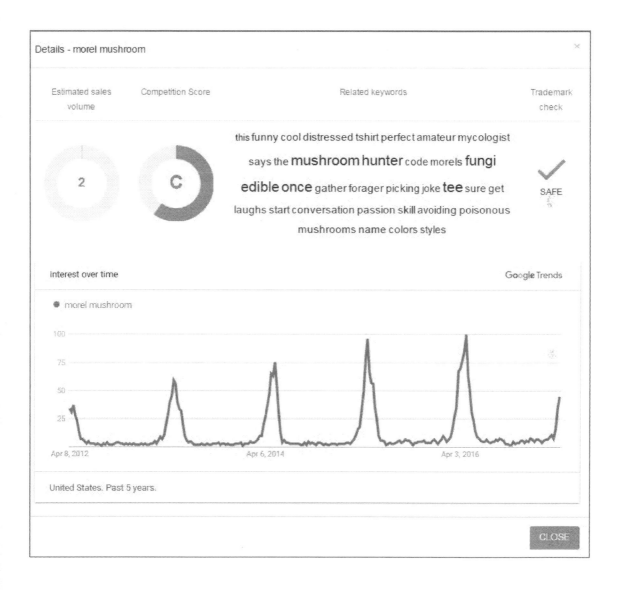

Advanced Competition Checker

As Merchants ourselves, we know how important statistics are. They give the perfect picture of how many designs are out there and being sold for certain keywords, what the competition looks like, and if the market has room for penetration. With Merch Informer's advanced competition checker, you will now be able to get a better idea of what kind of competition you are up against inside of Amazon's Algorithm.

Updated to include 20+ product categories for those selling print on demand products via the Shopify/Amazon integration. Merch by Amazon sellers can now expand their business fast!

Last results

Keywords/Phrase	Total results	Merch only results	Score (based on merch only results)	Seller who uses phrase as a brand
moms spaghetti	37	8	A	No
pasta	4165	121	C	Yes
mountain climbing	4623	200	D	Yes
bouldering	2582	124	C	Yes

DOWNLOAD RESULTS

Listing Optimizer

Having the best designs imaginable are not enough if you want to make sales. You need your product listings to be seen, which is why we recently released the product listing optimizer.

Split into two parts, the listing optimizer will both help you write better product descriptions and features based on relevant synonyms as well as help you tweak the pages you already have up. Cross reference ASINs and keywords to the product pages you have already created to see how well they are optimized.

Not taking the time to optimize your listings is leaving money on the table! Get your products in front of your buyers by running every listing through our optimizer for your best chance at success.

Organized Favorites

Long gone are the days of manually adding your ideas and inspiration to spreadsheets and trying to keep them organized. With our favorites feature, you can create organization trees to place designs that you want to improve upon in the future. This is especially useful by breaking down different niches, or keeping lists for separate designers.

Once you are satisfied with your choices, simply click on Download Product List and choose which options you want to be included in your download. You have the option to choose from:

- Title
- Image UR
- ASIN
- Price
- Features
- Description

You may choose which you want to include or not include in your spreadsheet and then click submit.

You now will have a perfectly organized spreadsheet to shoot of to your designer to do all the work!

MENU ≡

Categories

Pet T-Shirts

Dogs

Cats

Lizards

Birds

Holiday T-Shirts

Christmas

Santa

Snowing

Thanksgiving

Easter

Halloween

Witches

Scary

Nice

+ ADD CATEGORY   SAVE

DOWNLOAD PRODUCTS LIST

Merch Account Protection - Trademark Alerts

Trademark Alerts is finally here! We have heard the cries from the community.

How can you possibly keep track of what shirt slogans are safe when you have hundreds or thousands of shirts online?

What if one of your top selling phrases gets trademarked 3 months down the line, would you have any idea?

Now you will!

Trademark Alerts will monitor all your most important selling phrases in real time and alert you to any changes. If a phrase gets trademarked 5 months from now, you will know about it and be able to take preemptive action to keep your account safe!

No matter if you are selling on Merch by Amazon, or selling Merch on Seller Central via the Shopify Integration, keep your account protected with Merch Informer!

Trademarks		
Keywords/Phrase	Safe	Details
Facebook	✕	🛡
home.	✕	🛡
home	✕	🛡
Home.	✕	🛡
keep calm	✕	🛡
straight outta	✓	🛡
Twitter	✕	🛡
Youtube	✕	🛡

Merch Tracker

This module inside Merch Informer lets you track your own shirts or competitor tees for BSR/Price changes over time building beautiful graphs. Perfect for any marketing campaigns and analyzing data, which allows you to see exactly what kind of effect your efforts are having.

One of the most exciting aspects of this module is the ability to track your keywords on Amazon by keyword. You will be able to see exactly what position you are ranking in and how that changes after you optimize your listings.

Merch Hunter

Merch Informer recently released the long awaited *Merch Hunter* Module! This module will allow users to research by taking a look at the top 100 to top 1000 best selling shirts on Amazon.

You even have the ability to narrow down your research by picking 1-100k BSR or 100k and picking a keyword to really start niching down.

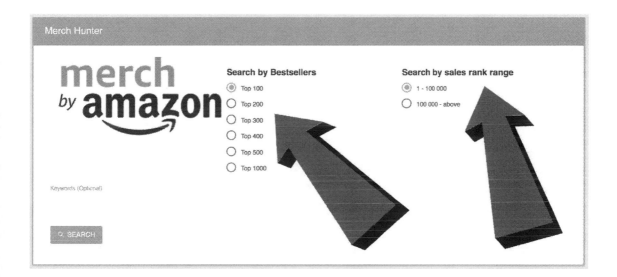

This is an incredibly powerful tool that let's you see the top-selling Merch By Amazon listings in order of sales rank (best sellers rank).

These lists are updated daily! This feature could almost be considered too powerful!

You can see the sales rank and expected monthly sales volume for the top-selling Merch listings.

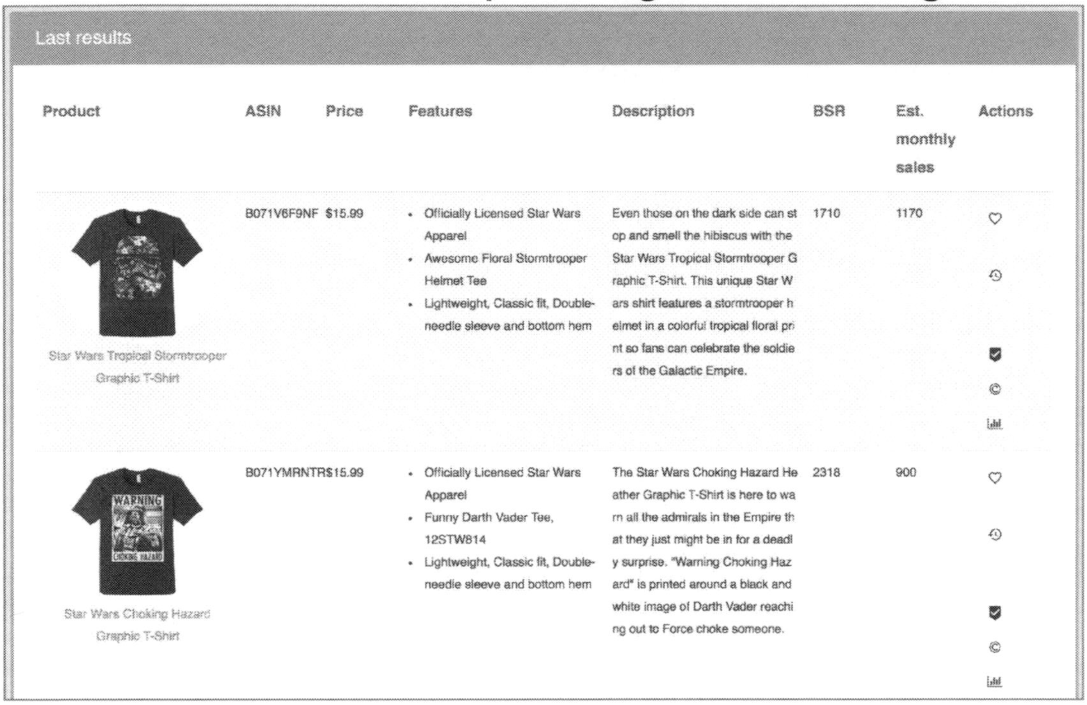

Last results							
Product	ASIN	Price	Features	Description	BSR	Est. monthly sales	Actions
Star Wars Tropical Stormtrooper Graphic T-Shirt	B071V6F9NF	$15.99	• Officially Licensed Star Wars Apparel • Awesome Floral Stormtrooper Helmet Tee • Lightweight, Classic fit, Double-needle sleeve and bottom hem	Even those on the dark side can stop and smell the hibiscus with the Star Wars Tropical Stormtrooper Graphic T-Shirt. This unique Star Wars shirt features a stormtrooper helmet in a colorful tropical floral print so fans can celebrate the soldiers of the Galactic Empire.	1710	1170	♡ ⟲ ☑ © �lıll
Star Wars Choking Hazard Graphic T-Shirt	B071YMRNTR	$15.99	• Officially Licensed Star Wars Apparel • Funny Darth Vader Tee, 12STW814 • Lightweight, Classic fit, Double-needle sleeve and bottom hem	The Star Wars Choking Hazard Heather Graphic T-Shirt is here to warn all the admirals in the Empire that they just might be in for a deadly surprise. "Warning Choking Hazard" is printed around a black and white image of Darth Vader reaching out to Force choke someone.	2318	900	♡ ⟲ ☑ © lıll

You can also add a keyword to your search to see seasonal or trending results.

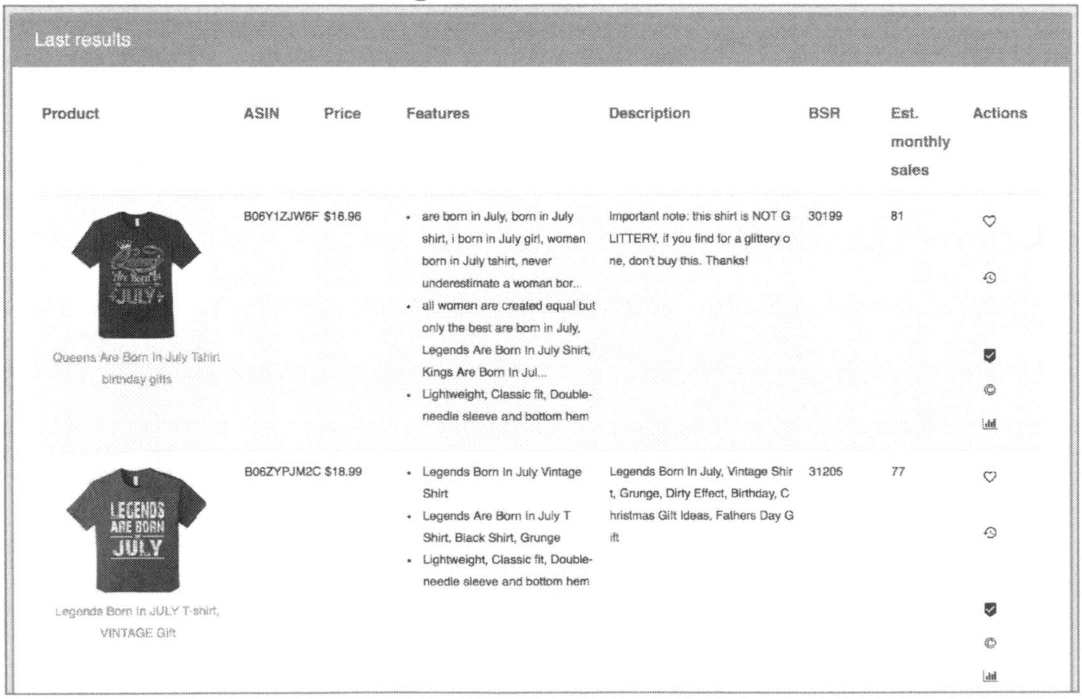

Last results							
Product	ASIN	Price	Features	Description	BSR	Est. monthly sales	Actions
Queens Are Born In July Tshirt birthday gifts	B06Y1ZJW6F	$16.96	• are born in July, born in July shirt, i born in July girl, women born in July tshirt, never underestimate a woman bor... • all women are created equal but only the best are born in July, Legends Are Born In July Shirt, Kings Are Born In Jul... • Lightweight, Classic fit, Double-needle sleeve and bottom hem	Important note: this shirt is NOT GLITTERY. if you find for a glittery one, don't buy this. Thanks!	30199	81	♡ ⟲ ☑ © lıll
Legends Born In JULY T-shirt, VINTAGE Gift	B06ZYPJM2C	$18.99	• Legends Born In July Vintage Shirt • Legends Are Born In July T Shirt, Black Shirt, Grunge • Lightweight, Classic fit, Double-needle sleeve and bottom hem	Legends Born In July, Vintage Shirt, Grunge, Dirty Effect, Birthday, Christmas Gift Ideas, Fathers Day Gift	31205	77	♡ ⟲ ☑ © lıll

Get Started With Merch Informer Today!

Sign Up

Sign up to Merch Informer by either paying monthly as you go, or prepay for 6 or 12 months. You even have the option to try it out risk free for 3 days.

Integrate

In order to use Merch Informer, you need to hook it up to the Amazon API. This is both free and easy! Make sure to watch the setup tutorial to fast track your setup.

Research

You are now all set up to start researching, getting ideas, and shooting off lists to your designers. Good luck!

BONUS!
Use code CG15 at signup
to save 15% FOR LIFE!

Fully Secure

Your information is safe and never shared. Product searches happen through the Amazon API so rest assured you are in good hands.

Lightning Fast

Compared to old methods of doing niche Merch research, we do it lightning fast saving you time!

Risk Free

We are so sure you will love our tool that you can try it risk free for 3 days to make sure that it is a good fit for your business.

Easy To Use

Merch Informer is incredibly easy to use. Make sure to read through the tutorials if you have any questions.

Full Support

If you ever have any issues getting set up, or come across something that is not working correctly, our support team will take care of you.

Continued Development

We are sellers ourselves! In order to create the best tool possible, development is continuing forward to add more features.

Realize Your Merch Potential

Amazon Merch research simplified and streamlined putting more money In your pocket

FREE 3 DAY TRIAL

All Merch By Amazon Listings (all in one place)

merchinformer.com/merch-amazon-listings

All Merch By Amazon Listings

Enter keyword or search term

Search

Use the search box to enter any keyword or phrase and see all of the Merch By Amazon search results. Works great on any phone or mobile device! Leave BLANK to see ALL Merch By Amazon shirts.

Social Media Research

merchinformer.com/search-social-media

Search Marketplaces

merchinformer.com/search-marketplaces

Search Marketplaces

merchinformer.com/search-marketplaces

Search Images

merchinformer.com/search-images

Search Images

merchinformer.com/search-images

4 - Facebook Groups

Merch By Amazon – MerchLife

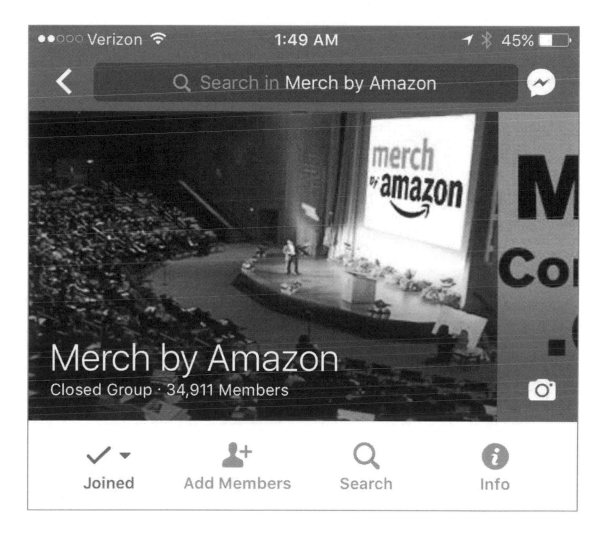

facebook.com/groups/MerchLife

Merch By Amazon - Merch Success 2.0

facebook.com/groups/MerchSuccess

5 - Design Hardware

The Apple iPad is an AMAZING device for making Merch By Amazon designs. There are several design apps that are only available on iOS devices. They are easy to learn and are capable of producing the 4500 x 5400 PNG files required by Merch By Amazon.

At the entry level is the iPad Mini which can be purchased for around $200.

The iPad Mini does not support the Apple Pencil (only iPad Pro models support the Apple Pencil).

You can use pressure sensitive styluses with the iPad Mini in order to get brush effects in certain apps. Take a look at the Adonit Pixel:

adonit.net/jot/pixel

iPad Pro + Pencil

If it's within your budget, the Apple iPad Pro (9.7" or 12.9") with the Apple Pencil will be a dream set up for making Merch By Amazon designs.

There are some great apps Like Over and Procreate that are capable of producing the 4500 x 5400 PNG files required by Merch By Amazon.

Wacom Tablets

The FIRST YouTube video from Adobe that teaches
Photoshop recommends getting a TABLET to use
for designing on your Mac or PC.

A quick Amazon search for Wacom tablet will bring
back some good ones.

Cintiq Pen Display Tablets

If it's within your budget, a standalone Cintiq display tablet is the premium set up for any type of design work done on a Mac or PC. Amazon carries the most popular models.

Seriously, within the first two minutes of Adobe's first YouTube video about Photoshop, they recommend getting a tablet.

See for yourself:

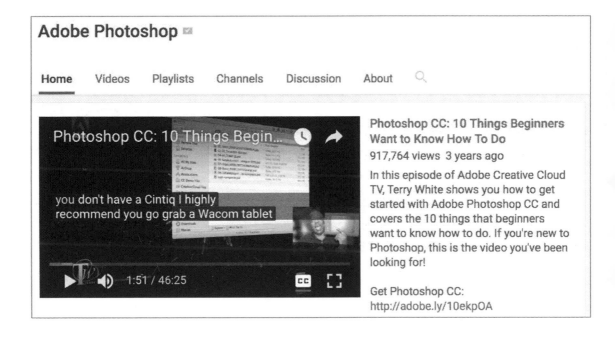

Adobe Photoshop YouTube Channel
youtube.com/user/Photoshop

6 - Desktop Software

Make-Merch.com

Q: What is Make-Merch?

A: Make-Merch is a membership site to enable users to quickly and easily create great looking designs for Merch by Amazon.

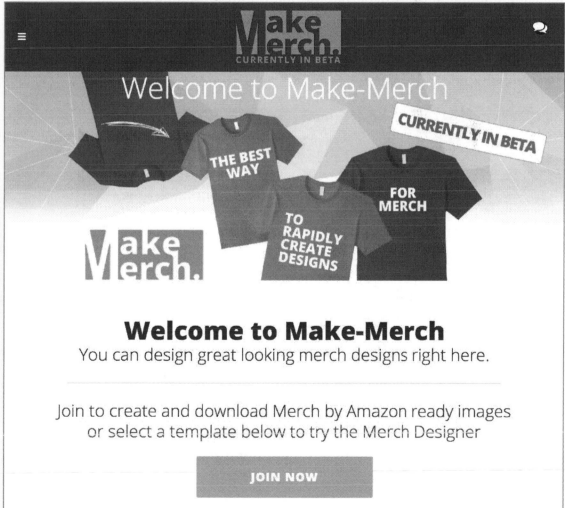

Some Inspiration From Our Team

Click on any design to use as a starting point for your own:

Q: Are the designs copyright free?

A: The Make-Merch team has made efforts to ensure that we only use images without any limitations on their use. Images are either created by our team or sourced from sites where the copyright is listed as CCO without any limitations on usage. If you find an image on Make-Merch that you believe is a violation, please inform us immediately.

Q: If I create a design using Make-Merch will Amazon automatically approve it?

A: Not necessarily. If the wording used in your design or the design itself does not meet Merch by Amazon's rules, your design will not be approved. If you need to prove to Amazon that the image itself is copyright free, please refer them to make-merch.com as the source. Please do not copy designs of other Make-Merch members.

Make-Merch currently has FIVE different Merch By Amazon t-shirt design templates as well as an awesome MOCKUP generator that you can use to make social media and other promotional images.

They are adding new features all the time as well.

STENCIL – MerchStencil.com

Stencil is now Merch By Amazon compatible!

Make designs in Stencil with dimensions 2250 x 2700 and then save as Retina @ 2x and you'll get a Merch-ready 4500 x 5400 PNG file!

Create UNLIMITED Merch By Amazon Designs for $18/month!

Three Steps to use Stencil

Step 1: Create custom canvas 2250 x 2700

Step 2: Click background and change to transparent background

Step 3: When downloading the finished design, choose Retina @2x for 4500x5400

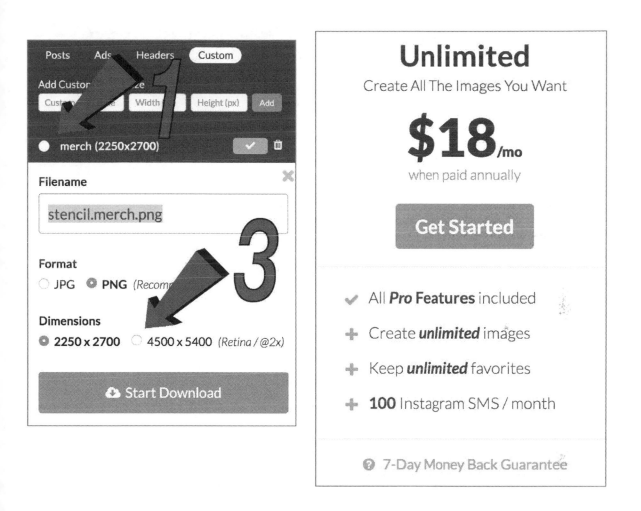

Are all the images and icons royalty-free?

Yes! In fact, they're all under a special public domain Creative Commons license called "CC0". That means you can use these photos however you want. We mean that literally. Personal, commercial, blog posts, posters...anything. Also, there's no attribution required whatsoever!

What is your refund policy?

If you're at all unhappy within 7 days of signing up, contact us for a full refund. Monthly recurring payments (other than your 1st month within 7 days) are non-refundable. However, if you're on our yearly plan, refunds are available 7 days from when your card is charged.

Create images faster & easier than ever before. Pick a background. Add some text. No biggie.

1,110,000+ background photos

More royalty-free "CC0" images than you'll know what to do with! Hundreds of new photos added every week!

600+ Amazing Templates

Create beautiful images even faster with our PRO templates, ready to be edited.

Upload & Store Multiple Logos

Upload & store every variation of your logo or different logos if you're creating visuals for different brands.

100,000+ Quotes

Make inspiring quote images in seconds by searching through our collection of quotes right in Stencil.

2,000+ Google Web Fonts

Find the perfect font for your image by using any of Google's thousands of web fonts!

Upload your own fonts

Match your brand perfectly by uploading your own fonts directly to Stencil and use them in all your visuals.

200,000+ Icons & Graphics

Vector icons from The Noun Project and EmojiOne right at your finger tips, royalty-free and safe to use however you want (personal or commercial).

36+ custom sizes for all your needs

We've done all the research and pre-loaded the optimal sizes for social networks, ads, blog posts and more. Not enough? Create your own (like Merch By Amazon!

Easy-to-use Chrome Extension

Create images 'on-the-go' while browsing the web using our amazing Chrome Extension.

https://chrome.google.com/webstore/detail/stencil/hgmhphfbdfbkokcfajipbmkcakmmepeb

Instantly add text to any image - just right click!

The Stencil Chrome extension lets you highlight text anywhere on the web and turn it into an image instantly. See an image you want to add some text to? Just right-click any image and select Stencil.

Then you can start creating and customizing your image!

Get a free trial of Stencil at:
MerchStencil.com

MerchDesigner.com

MerchDesigner is included FREE for members of The RiverBank! http://River-Bank.com

Merch Designer is currently a web-based application for making Merch By Amazon designs. You can use any of the included artwork or upload your own.

You can add text, change fonts, resize, and more. Merch Designer is great for making simple Merch By Amazon t-shirt designs quickly and with no graphic design experience. Files are exported as 4500 x 5400 PNG files.

PlaceIt.net Smart Templates

placeit.net/c/apparel/?f_types=design_template&f_d
evices=Design%20Template

Make your own t-shirt design with this web-based t-shirt design template application and rock the market! All you have to do is use the menu on the right to modify the background and the graphic. Don't forget to choose their color! Then use the menu on the left to add your own text; you can change each line's font and color,

This link with get you a 15% discount from PlaceIt.net:
placeit.refersion.com/c/d744c

PlaceIt provides a very versatile template Merch By Amazon T-shirt designs! The menu on the left will let you change the text, color, and font. Don't forget to choose your graphic and background; you are also able to modify their colors.

Here are some more examples of editable PlaceIt t-shirt templates:

https://placeit.net/c/design-templates/?f_devices=T-Shirt%20Design&h=2

Make a Sports Logo for Your Team with PlaceIt!
Create your own sports logo in seconds!
https://placeit.net/c/design-templates/?f_devices=Logo&f_tags=Sports&h=3

Sports Team Logo Maker – Human Characters

Start using Placeit to design a sports logo in a creative and beautiful way! The menu on the right side of the...

Sports Logo Maker – Cartoonish Animals

If you are looking to design a team logo, you've reached the right place! Placeit has an excellent tool for you ...

Sports Logo Maker – Aggressive Animals

Looking for a way to design a sports logo? Use Placeit! You could use this awesome sports team logo maker a...

Gaming Logo – Fantasy Creatures

This gaming logo maker is a great choice for you to start making your esports logo in a simple and...

Basketball Logo Maker

Looking for a way to create an awesome basketball logo in a super-easy and beautiful way? Use Placeit!...

Baseball Logo Maker

Take a look at this baseball logo generator by Placeit, use it to create your own baseball logo designs in a...

Football Logo Maker

Take a look at this beautiful football logo maker by Placeit, it's a gorgeous tool that you can use to create your...

Soccer Logo Maker

Make a soccer logo in a simple and beautiful way! Use Placeit to create your own custom soccer logo and...

Sports Logo Generator – Capital Letter Badge

Take a look at this awesome sports logo maker from Placeit! It's a really cool tool that you can use to start...

Photoshop

adobe.com/products/photoshop.html

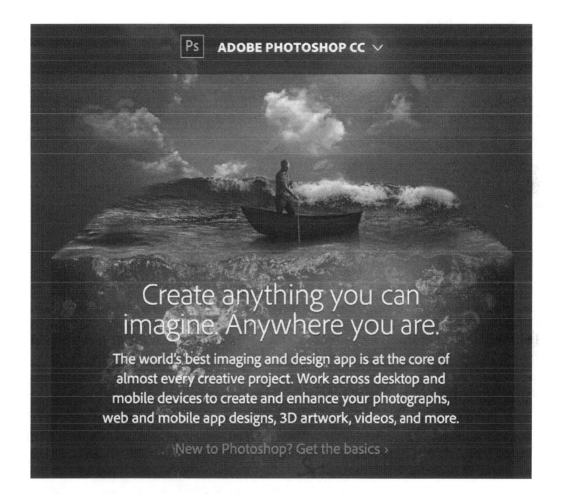

Photoshop CC can be purchased for just $9.99/month. It is a very inexpensive way to get started. YouTube and Adobe both offer TONS of free videos to help you learn Photoshop. There are also online courses.

YouTube - youtube.com/user/Photoshop

Illustrator

adobe.com/products/illustrator.html

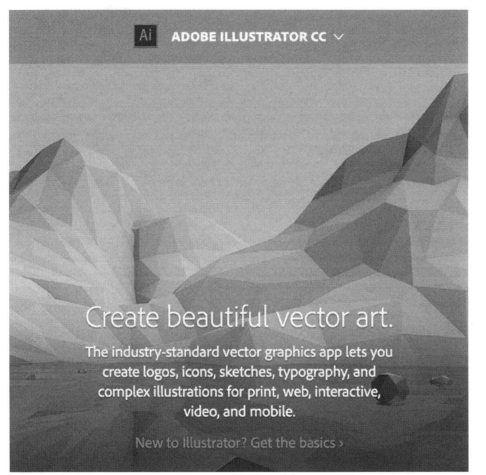

Illustrator can be purchased for just $19.99/month. Another inexpensive very inexpensive way to get started. YouTube and Adobe both offer TONS of free videos to help you learn Illustrator. There are also online courses.

If you are starting **100% FRESH** with no experience with Photoshop or Illustrator, I recommend learning Illustrator. I say this because of how many of my professional design friends use Illustrator over Photoshop.

7 - Mobile Design Apps

Over - madewithover.com

Over is currently only on iOS devices but it is seriously SO GOOD that I recommend that people buy an iOS device (even if just an iPad Mini or iPod Touch) just to use the Over app for Merch By Amazon.

There are not many apps that support the creation and export of 4500 x 5400 PNG files but the Over app handles them like a champ!

Over PRO

Powerful Tools

Quickly create professional quality content. Save time and money.

Huge Library

Get noticed with 100,000+ ready-made graphics, fonts & images.

Easy to Learn

Not a designer? No problem! Over PRO makes it easy for anyone to create.

TRY FREE FOR 7 DAYS

Subscribe annually and save 60%

TOP IN-APP PURCHASES

1.	OverPro	$9.99
2.	Fonts for Pictures	$2.99
3.	PRO PHOTO EDITOR TOOLKIT	$2.99
4.	Big Font & Graphics Bundle	$2.99
5.	Cursive Fonts Pack	$1.99
6.	Funky Fonts Pack	$1.99
7.	Drop Shadow Text Effects	$1.99
8.	Add Artwork, Text & Images	$1.99
9.	Compliment Filled Text Pack	$1.99
10.	Blend Mask Effects, Text, Artwork & Images	$1.99

Over PRO is a must-have. It's very powerful and inexpensive.

Download on the App Store

Another great thing about the Over app is that they have tons of resources and tutorials to help you get the most out of the app and help you become a great designer!

This TEN VIDEO series will get you up and running with the incredible Over app! Use Over to make your Merch By Amazon designs from your iPhone or iPad!

You can also view this list on Facebook here:

facebook.com/notes/merch-by-amazon-merch-life/over/1714620231912808

Full TEN VIDEO Playlist:
youtube.com/playlist?list=PLGy1_FmEQT1Kf8Kj EZ0PI0OP2GTNzw7pn

Or view each video using the links below:

1: Downloading the Over App
https://youtu.be/l41EaaTwzP8

2: Over vs. Over Pro
https://youtu.be/M3k8czxxkQ4

3: Setting 4500 x 5400 Dimensions
https://youtu.be/lk-QWXMsE3M

4: Adding & Editing Images
https://youtu.be/OpnhQweOA30

5: Adding & Editing Text
https://youtu.be/Tl6od3S0dBE

6: Adding & Editing Shapes
https://youtu.be/-D9mimjs9lc

7: Importing Fonts
https://youtu.be/ytBPFWQ7BOs

8: Importing Images (Zip Files)
https://youtu.be/J5tBl0nsC_0

9: Importing Images (Dropbox Links)
https://youtu.be/K0u-kXwluYw

10: Saving as PNG
https://youtu.be/6xaA--41lPs

Dimensions Reference Chart

Over

SHIRT: 4500 x 5400 PNG FILE
72 - 300 DPI, under 25MB

POST: 2048 x 1536

Profile Picture (1:1): 360 x 360
Profile/Page Header (Desktop): 828 x 315
Profile/Page Header (Mobile): 282 x 465
Group Header: 801 x 250
Event Header: 784 x 295

twitter

TWEET (3:2): 2048 x 1365

Profile Picture (1:1): 500 x 500
Profile Header: 1500 x 500

Pinterest

PIN (2:3): 1365 x 2048

Profile Picture (1:1): 600 x 600
Board Cover: 736 x 498

Instagram

POST (1:1): 2048 x 2048

Profile Picture (1:1): 180 x 180

Other Print On Demand Sites

	Dimensions	Resolution	Filetype
Merch By Amazon	4500x5400	72-300	PNG
Cafepress	2000x2000	200	PNG
Teespring	3000x3000	72-120	PNG
Zazzle	ANY	150+	PNG
Teepublic	1500x1995	150+	PNG
Spreadshirt	2200x2200	200	AI, .EPS
Gearbubble	1000x1000	144	PNG
Threadless	4200x4800	300	PNG
Redbubble	2400x3200	72+	PNG
Viralstyle	3000x3000	72+	PNG
Sunfrog	2400x3200	72+	PNG
CustomizedGirl	1000x1000	72+	PNG
Society6	3300x5100	72+	JPG
Represent	4000x4000	300	PNG

Other Sizes

Etsy	2048x500
YouTube (HD)	1920x1080
LinkedIn (3:2)	2048x1365
iPhone 5	640x1136
iPhone 6(S)	750x1334
iPhone 6(S)+	1242x2208
iPhone 7	750x1334
iPhone 7+	1920x1080
38mm iWatch	272x340
42mm iWatch	319x390

Procreate - procreate.art

Create beautiful sketches - Tools as powerful as your ideas

With Procreate's remarkable pencils, you'll be creating beautiful sketches in no time. With the power of your iPad, your concepts can flow as fast as your ideas.

Inspiring paintings without the mess - Everything from classical to digital

Carry an unlimited library of brushes with you wherever you go. Procreate gives you a natural and fluid painting experience powered by Silica: the fastest 64-bit painting engine on iOS.

Free yourself from the desktop - Sensational advances for illustrators

Procreate has all the tools you need to create breathtaking illustrations; including an advanced layer system, massive canvas resolutions, 64-bit color, and stunning cinema quality effects.

The art of performance - Designed exclusively for iPad

Procreate is a 64-bit performance powerhouse built only for iPad. Discover just how easy it is to create richly detailed artworks anywhere you are.

https://itunes.apple.com/us/app/procreate-sketch-paint-create./id425073498?mt=8

Amaziograph - amaziograph.com

With **Amaziograph** everybody is an Artist!

Amaziograph allows you to create amazing drawings on your iPad. Just $0.99

Amaziograph Features

Symmetries

Amaziograph applies symmetries to everything you draw.

Creating a symmetric image is easy: choose the type of graph you want and then draw! You can see how your tessellation changes as you draw. Whatever you draw, it looks beautiful.

- **Mirror**
- Rotation
- 2-mirror kaleidoscope
- 3-mirror kaleidoscope
- Tiles

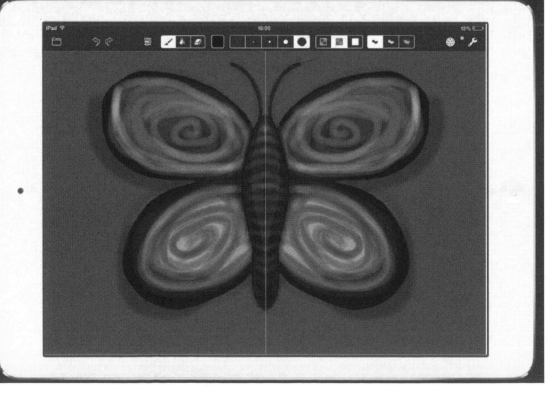

Not only does Amaziograph allow you to use a symmetry while drawing, but it also enables you to change or turn off the symmetry in the process of drawing. Furthermore, you can configure the symmetry grid as you like.

iOrnament

Website:
http://www.science-to-touch.com/en/iOrnament.html

App:
https://itunes.apple.com/us/app/iornament-draw-creative-geometry-art/id534529876?mt=8

First of all iOrnament is a drawing app! You draw simple strokes with your finger or the Apple Pencil - iOrnament repeats them automatically according to the rules of a selected symmetry group. By just drawing a few strokes fascinating patterns emerge. People of almost all ages starting from 3 year old kids up to scientifically or artistically interested grownups can spend hours in the creative process of creating ornaments, tilings or infinite knots. iOrnament lets you creativity flow, unexpected twists appear while you are drawing follow them to see where they lead. iOrnament is at the same time relaxing, meditative, scientific, artistic, structured, hypnotic, fun and educational.

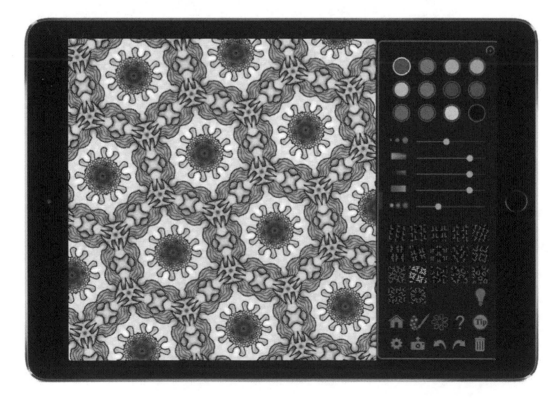

Affinity Photo (iPad)

Website:
https://affinity.serif.com/en-us/photo/ipad

App:
https://itunes.apple.com/us/app/affinity-photo/id1117941080?mt=8

Professional photo editing on iPad

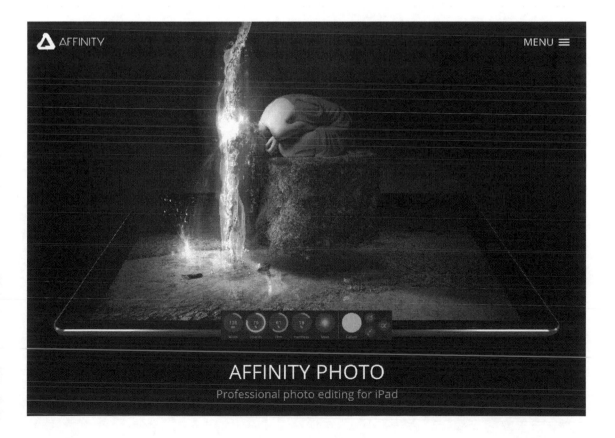

AFFINITY PHOTO
Professional photo editing for iPad

Developed without compromise, Affinity Photo for iPad is the first full-blown, truly professional photo-editing tool to make its way onto the Apple tablet. Built from exactly the same back-end as our award-winning desktop version, and fully optimized to harness the full power of the iPad's hardware and touch capabilities. Affinity Photo for iPad offers an incredibly fast, powerful and immersive experience whether you are at home, in the studio or on the move.

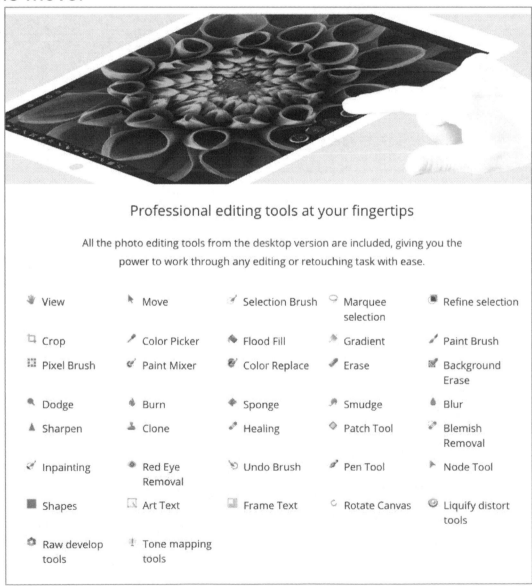

Professional editing tools at your fingertips

All the photo editing tools from the desktop version are included, giving you the power to work through any editing or retouching task with ease.

✋ View	↖ Move	Selection Brush	Marquee selection	Refine selection
Crop	Color Picker	Flood Fill	Gradient	Paint Brush
Pixel Brush	Paint Mixer	Color Replace	Erase	Background Erase
Dodge	Burn	Sponge	Smudge	Blur
Sharpen	Clone	Healing	Patch Tool	Blemish Removal
Inpainting	Red Eye Removal	Undo Brush	Pen Tool	Node Tool
Shapes	Art Text	Frame Text	Rotate Canvas	Liquify distort tools
Raw develop tools	Tone mapping tools			

Assembly

Website:
http://assemblyapp.co

App:
https://itunes.apple.com/us/app/assem
bly-graphic-design-
for/id1024210402?mt=8

Create Graphics, Stickers and Logos

Produce quality work in half the time.

Professional Output. SVG. PDF.

Powerful tools found in high end design suites.

Design with Building Blocks

Combine shapes to create complex compositions.

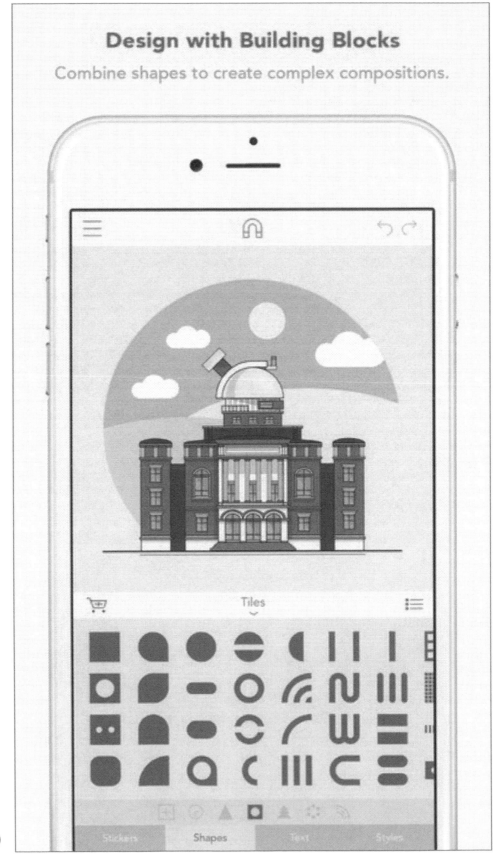

Add Text to your designs

Beautiful fonts to fit any style.

Cameraxis

App: https://itunes.apple.com/us/app/cameraxis-graphic-design-photo-editing/id925547507?mt=8

TAKE TYPOGRAPHY TO THE NEXT LEVEL

INFUSE YOUR LIFE WITH WITH ACTION. DON'T WAIT IT FOR HAPPEN. MAKE YOUR OWN FUTURE. MAKE YOUR OWN HOPE. MAKE YOUR OWN LOVE. AND WHATEVER YOUR BELIEFS, HONOR YOUR CREATOR, NOT BY PASSIVELY WAITING FOR GRACE TO COME DOWN FROM UPON HIGH, BUT BY DOING WHAT YOU CAN TO MAKE GRACE HAPPEN YOURSELF, RIGHT NOW, RIGHT DOWN HERE ON EARTH. -Bradley Whitford

750+ FULLY CUSTOMIZABLE GRAPHIC TEMPLATES

CREATE PROFESSIONAL DESIGNS IN SECONDS

Design Font Apps (MerchApps.com)

https://www.designfontapps.com

CREATE INSPIRING TEXT IMAGES IN SECONDS!

VINTAGE FONT

FEATURES:

Fast and easy to use

Makes vintage text designs

Save as transparent PNGs

Save as 4500 x 5400 pixels

Commercial use art + font

Import your own fonts

SUPERB FOR SOCIAL MEDIA AND BLOGS

CREATE INSPIRING TEXT IMAGES IN JUST SECONDS!

DESIGN FONT

FEATURES:

Fast and easy to use

Makes super text designs

Save as transparent PNGs

Save as 4500 x 5400 pixels

Commercial use art + font

Import your own fonts

SUPERB FOR SOCIAL MEDIA AND BLOGS!

CREATE AWESOME MUG + T-SHIRT DESIGNS!

CIRCLE FONT

CREATE FAST + EASY CIRCLE FONTS

FEATURES:

Fast and easy to use
Beautiful circle designs
Transparent backgrounds
4500 x 5400 size images
Commercial use font + art
Import your own fonts

INCLUDES A FAST 'MERCH' RESIZER!

RESIZE IMAGES

RESIZE PNG FILES AND KEEP THEIR TRANSPARENCY!

FEATURES:

Fast and easy to use
Resize PNG & JPG pics
Transparent backgrounds
4500 x 5400 sized images
Resize in bulk
Merch T-Shirt Resizer

118

GET AMAZING DISTRESSED EFFECTS!

DISTRESSED FONT

FEATURES:

Fast and easy to use

Distress transparent pics

Make your text amazing!

Saves to original size

Distress in bulk

Great for shirt designs

DISTRESS THE TEXT IN YOUR TRANSPARENT T-SHIRT PNGS

AMAZING PATTERN FX TO CHOOSE FROM

PATTERN FONT

FEATURES:

Fast and easy to use

Make your PNGs 3D

Create amazing FX!

Save to original size

Great for shirt designs

OVER THE TEXT IN YOUR TRANSPARENT T-SHIRT PNGS WITH AWESOME PATTERNS!

119

ICON FONT

ADD ICONS TO ANY IMAGE

MAKE COOL DESIGNS WITHOUT NEEDING A DESIGNER!

FEATURES:

Fast and easy to use
Add icons to any image
Save as original size
and PNG / JPG format
Lots of colors
Great for text designs

CLOUD FONT

CREATE BEAUTIFUL WORD CLOUD IMAGES

EXPORT TRANSPARENT PNG IMAGES, PERFECT FOR MERCH AND POD

FEATURES:

Fast and easy to use
Design great word clouds
Transparent backgrounds
4500 x 5400 size images
Commercial use font
Import your own fonts

Canva - canva.com

Canva is a great application for both web-based designs and iOS devices. They don't currently support Merch By Amazon 4500 x 5400 dimensions, but Canva can still be useful for making design elements or even just to play around with and get an eye for good design.

Be sure to read their full licensing terms here: about.canva.com/license-agreements

Word Swag - <u>wordswag.co</u>

Word Swag Samples

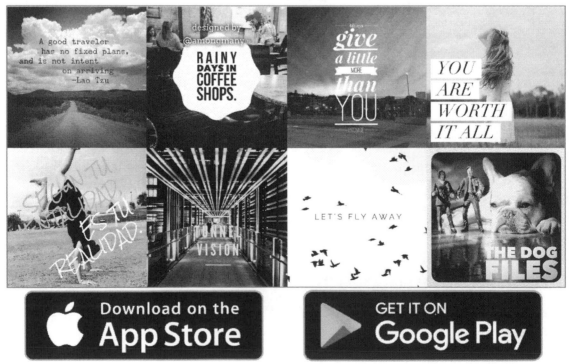

Logo Maker

https://itunes.apple.com/us/app/logo-maker-logo-creator-to-create-logo-design/id1143390028?mt=8

Logo Maker is the simplest app to create logo on your iPhone, iPad and iPod. Create stunning logos, icons, symbols, posters in just a few clicks.

Logo Maker help you visualize and communicate the value of your brand without any design experience from your side.

iOS Eraser App

This app helps to remove the background of any picture of yours and maintain transparency with just few taps. Just touch where you want to remove. "Target" function removes the area of similar color automatically.

https://itunes.apple.com/gb/app/background-eraser-superimpose-photo-editor-cut-out/id815072622?mt=8

#PNG/ JPEG File Selection - Selecting type of output picture:

(PNG for transparent background or JPEG for white background)

8 - Merch Design Services

MerchPower – MerchPower.com

MerchPower is a design service for Merch By Amazon that allows members to make detailed requests to a team of professional designers. Requests can be made by email or through an online request form.

All files and communication are handled through enterprise-level messaging and file management software.

Request Form

Fill out a request form on your client's behalf. Clients may also submit request details to requests@inbound.jarhq.com

Select A Client *

Select A Client *

Select A Client User *

Select A Client User *

Request name or subject *

Request name or subject *

Details of your request *

Details of your request *

Final size or dimensions *

Final size or dimensions *

Who is the target audience for this design? *

Who is the target audience for this design? *

Share any links to designs you like here. Hit tab after each link

Share any links to designs you like here. Hit tab after each link

What are you NOT looking for?

What are you NOT looking for?

Client Attachments. Select file(s) or drag and drop onto button

Choose Files | No file chosen

☐ I have uploaded all final copy and resources *

Submit Request

Requests   Team   Clients   [Search]   Chris Green ⌄

CG C Green   29 days ago

Details:

make it badass

Final Dimensions:

4500 x 5400, PNG

Target Audience:

true players

Not Looking For:

lame sauce

Attached Files:

puffpufflifestyle.png

halloween.png

puffpuff.png

Brandon Ortega   28 days ago **BO**

'Awesome T-shirt' 4500 x 5400, PNG and a mock up have been added.   Let me know what you think!

Click here to Reply or add a Note

---

test shirt request
#1

[Files]

Requestor Info

👤 C Green

🗋 TEST ACCOUNTS

📅 7/18/2017

Request Details

[Update]

🗓 Status

[Open]

👥 Group

[DESIGNERS   × ▾]

👤 Designer

[Brandon Ortega   × ▾]

🏷 Tags

[▾]

📅 Due Date

[   ]

Archive Request

Files   Current Uploads   [New Folder]   [Upload]

Merch.co ❯ Client Companies ❯ TEST ACCOUNTS ❯ Requests ❯ #1

📁 **Client Attachments**
   Jul 18, 2017 10:32 AM ● 7.7 MB

awesome t-shirt.png
Jul 19, 2017 10:24 AM ● 1.3 MB

👕 **awesome tshirt MOCKUP.png**
   Jul 19, 2017 10:24 AM ● 616.3 KB

awesome tshirt MOCKUP.png

[Copy Public Link]   [Download]   [Delete]

[Close]

MerchReady – **MerchReady.com**

MerchReady is full service design company offering 'Merch Ready' designs. Not only are their designs ready for Merch by Amazon, but they will also provide title, and 2 bullet points - all researched by their team.

9 - Graphic Design Services

Design Pickle - DesignPickle.com

Try out Design Pickle by visiting MerchPickle.com and using code CG2017 to save 30%! They have a 14-day no-risk trial!

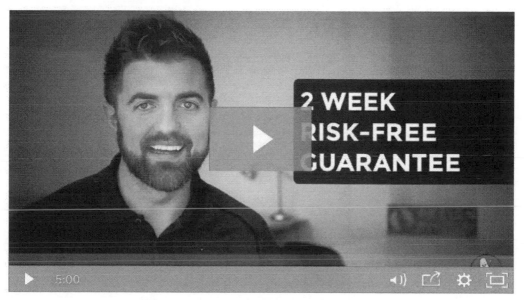

GRAPHIC DESIGNS FOR EVERY BUSINESS

FROM CMO'S TO SOLO-ENTREPRENEURS,
THOUSANDS OF CLIENTS HAVE FOUND THEIR
PERSONAL DESIGNER WITH DESIGN PICKLE.

SEE OUR MOST RECENT WORK

PROFESSIONAL BY DESIGN

DESIGN PICKLE IS A GRAPHIC DESIGN SERVICE BUILT FROM
THE GROUND UP TO HELP YOU BE MORE CREATIVE ON A DAILY
BASIS.

Get matched with one of our full-time, professional designers.

Our team works fast - your designer works daily on your requests.

JPG, PNG, PDF & Adobe files included. You 100% own the work!

Unlimited requests & unlimited revisions mean there's no limit to your creativity.

Need help with your designs? Our support team is happy to help.

Our flat-rate pricing means you pay the same price every month, no matter what!

Making a request is easy!
Just email request@designpickle.com,
or complete the form below.

Name of request

Details of request

Final size or dimensions

Who is the target audience for this design?

We love inspiration. Share any links to designs you like here.

What are you NOT looking for?

ADD FILES...

Upload any files we'll need for the design here.

☐ I've described or uploaded all final copy and content for this design

PICKLE IT!

131

You read that right!

If you are interested in Design Pickle and have any questions about how to best use their unlimited graphic design services with Merch By Amazon, just send me an email to chris@merch.co to schedule a 100% FREE, no-strings-attached Design Pickle coaching call!

I have my own Design Pickle account that I use for Merch By Amazon designs and I can share with you the best way to work with Design Pickle designers.

RaftShirt - raftshirt.com

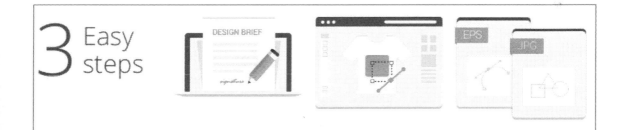

3 Easy steps

Get started by telling us a few details to help us create your perfect t-shirt.

Our experienced illustrators will design a unique t-shirt to suit your event or business.

The t-shirt will be available within 24 to 48 hours.

STARTER	PROFESSIONAL	ADVANCED
$13	**$17**	**$24**
Unique one of a kind design	Unique one of a kind design	Unique one of a kind design
Simple typography based design up to 3 colors	Vintage effect, premium typography	Vintage effect, premium typography & graphic illustration
3000 x 3000 HQ transparent front PNG	3000 x 3000 HQ transparent front PNG	3000 x 3000 HQ transparent front PNG
Unlimited Revisions	Unlimited Revisions	Unlimited Revisions
Optimised for Teespring	Optimised for Teespring	Optimised for Teespring
Optimized for Merch by Amazon	Optimized for Merch by Amazon	Optimized for Merch by Amazon
Fast Delivery	Super-Fast Delivery	Super-Fast Delivery
Money Back Guarantee	Money Back Guarantee	Money Back Guarantee
Buy Now	Buy Now	Buy Now

Undullify - undullify.com

Graphic design, but better

Our monthly subscription service gives you unlimited small graphic design tasks. It's simple, affordable, and headache-free. With Undullify, you'll also get these great features...

Unlimited small design tasks

Send us an unlimited number of small design tasks. A small task is any design task that we can complete within 30 minutes.

Unlimited number of revisions

Because we want you to love our work as much as we do, we don't place a hard limit on the number of revisions you can request.

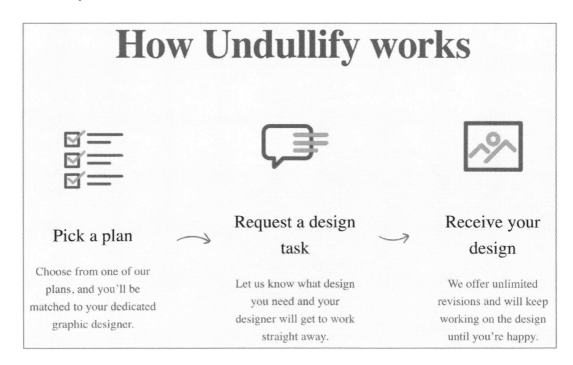

How Undullify works

Pick a plan

Choose from one of our plans, and you'll be matched to your dedicated graphic designer.

Request a design task

Let us know what design you need and your designer will get to work straight away.

Receive your design

We offer unlimited revisions and will keep working on the design until you're happy.

Flocksy – flocksy.com

ON DEMAND CUSTOM GRAPHIC DESIGN AND WEBSITE HELP STARTING AT $199/MONTH

Unlimited projects with quick turnaround times. All work is managed by a Dedicated Project Manager who makes sure all your projects are done on time and correctly. **100% money back guarantee!**

HOW FLOCKSY WORKS

What we do here at Flocksy can be boiled down to ten words: we're your on demand graphic design and website help team. When you need work done you just log into your account, start a request and we'll get it completed quickly, professionally, and most importantly, beautifully.

It really couldn't be simpler:

1. You need graphic design or website work done
2. We do the work.
3. You smile.
4. Repeat as needed.

WHAT IS INCLUDED WHEN I SIGN UP?

☑ Dedicated Project Manager based in the USA

☑ 7-day money back guarantee

☑ A professional graphic design team that will create just about anything

☑ Guaranteed fast turnaround times

☑ Programmers to help maintain your website

☑ Easy to use project management board

☑ Amazing customer service

☑ No contracts

BrandStrong - brandstrong.co

Brandstrong was formed to create a simple solution – you need designs done, for anything and everything, and you don't want it to cost the earth.

For a fixed monthly fee, we provide unlimited graphic design for anything – from leaflets and flyers, to logos and brochures. From book covers to Facebook covers, if it requires a design, we do it.

And we don't limit the task to be less than 30 minutes, or an hour – if you have a multi page brochure that needs designing and it takes 3 hours, that's fine.

If you have a need for a logo, and there's a bit of back and forth to tweak it, also fine – no limits on the revisions.

Think of it like a membership to an awesome design club – you pay your fee, and you can use it for whatever design needs you have.

10 – Design & Font Resources

Brandi Lea is a Graphic Designer who is familiar with the Merch By Amazon program. All of her graphic packs on Creative Market can be used to create Merch By Amazon designs!

creativemarket.com/brandilea

Big Hand Drawn ... $24
by Brandi Lea D......

Hand Drawn Chri... $15
by Brandi Lea D......

1000 Hand Drawn.. $15
by Brandi Lea D......

Hand Drawn Arro... $5
by Brandi Lea D... i...

Hand Drawn Circ... $5
by Brandi Lea D... i...

150 Hand-Drawn ... $10
by Brandi Lea D......

55 Pairs of Hand-... $10
by Brandi Lea D......

Hand Drawn Flor... $5
by Brandi Lea D... i...

Hand Drawn Laur... $5
by Brandi Lea D... i...

Wreaths for Craft... $5
by Brandi Lea D... i...

Hand Drawn Wre... $5
by Brandi Lea D... i...

$2 Sale - 30 Strok... $2
by Brandi Lea D... i...

Hajime Script $12
by Brandi Lea D......

The Huge Digital ... $19
by Brandi Lea D......

Patterned Hearts... $5
by Brandi Lea D... i...

Cat Silhouettes f... $5
by Brandi Lea D... i...

Bird Silhouettes f... $5
by Brandi Lea D... i...

Deer Silhouettes ... $5
by Brandi Lea D... i...

https://www.thefancydeal.com/downloads/tshirts-designs-bundle/?ref=1435

What You Get:

200 vector designs in Ai & SVG
Editable layers and text in Ai files in Adobe Illustrator

Extended license: All these designs are in layered AI file format.
You need to open it in Adobe Illustrator and you'll see all layers
and you can replace or delete some layers and customize these
designs for your projects. You can edit all texts in Adobe Illustrator.

Here are just four examples from the 200 EDITABLE designs from this bundle.

They also have other great design bundles!

Creative Market - creativemarket.com

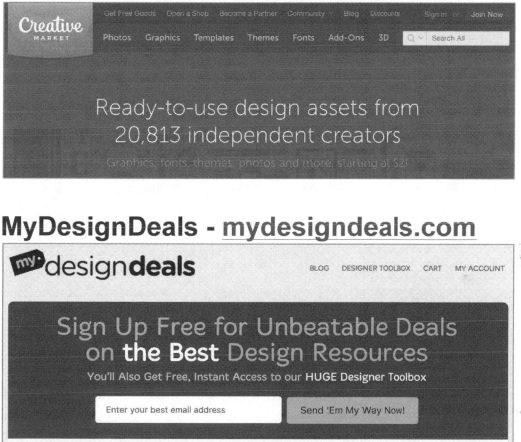

MyDesignDeals - mydesigndeals.com

Design Bundles - designbundles.net

Font Bundles - fontbundles.net

Welcome to FontBundles.net - The Home of all Things Design

Whether you are a handmade paper crafter, an Etsy seller, a card maker, a Cricut Lover, a silhouette crafter or any kind of creative person we are sure you will find Font Bundles a fantastic resource and excellent value for money.

We have gone to the ends of the earth and back again, sourcing the very best fonts and designs from some of the most creative and talented font designers in the world today. We then had the pleasure of bundling them up, creating the packaging and making them available to you at some seriously reduced prices. Typically with our bundles you can save as much as 96% off the RRP. That's huge!

As well as our ludicrously cheap font bundles we also offer a complete Font Marketplace consisting of some of the very best
142

typography fonts to grace the online world. Whether its calligraphy fonts you are looking for, script fonts, brush fonts or just regular fonts we have got you covered. Be sure to check out our Daily Font Deal and featured Font Bundle for even more discounted design work.

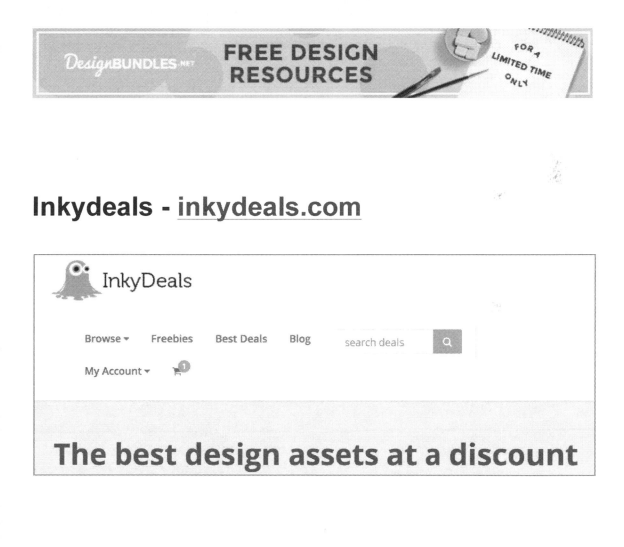

Inkydeals - inkydeals.com

The Hungry JPEG - thehungryjpeg.com

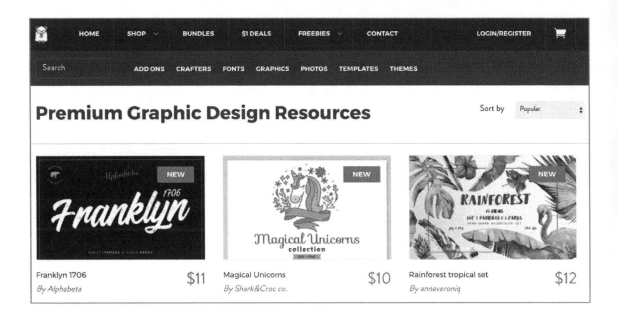

Pixelo - pixelo.net

DesignCuts - designcuts.com

PixelBuddha - pixelbuddha.net

Pixelbuddha

— We're passionate about creating free and premium resources for professional community.

24 May 2017

The Comprehensive Texture and Patterns Collection

Have a brief break and check the most varied textures and patterns bundle our friends from Design Cuts have ever made for you.

23 May 2017

3d Space Landscape Background

We're amazed to bring more space enigma to your artworks. Indeed inspired by plasma, washing the land of an enigmatic planet, these backgrounds will not leave your followers indifferent.

GraphicRiver - graphicriver.net

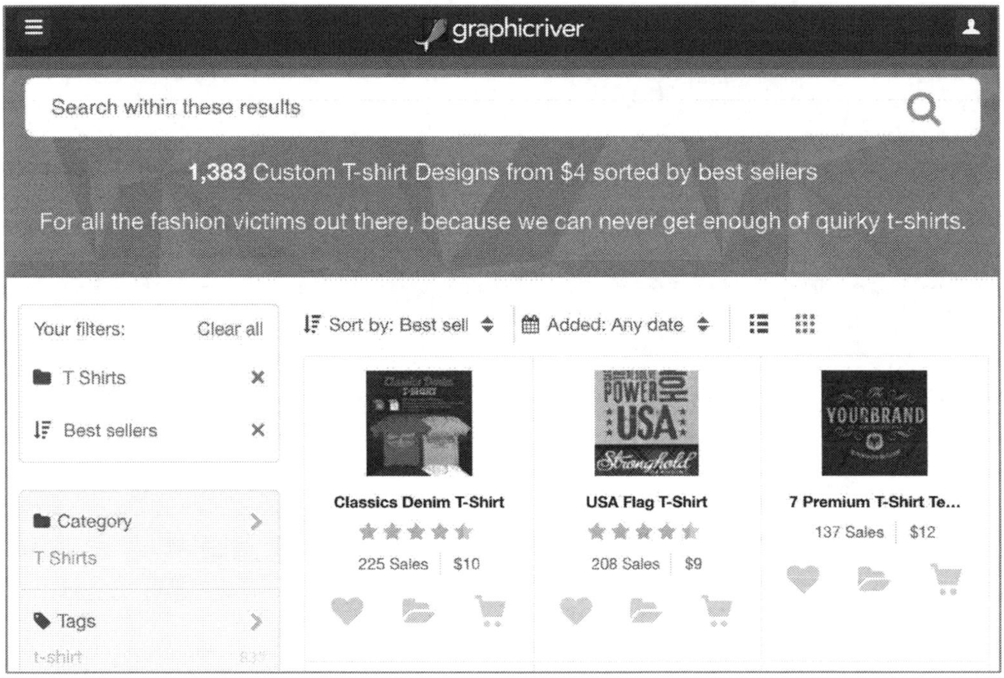

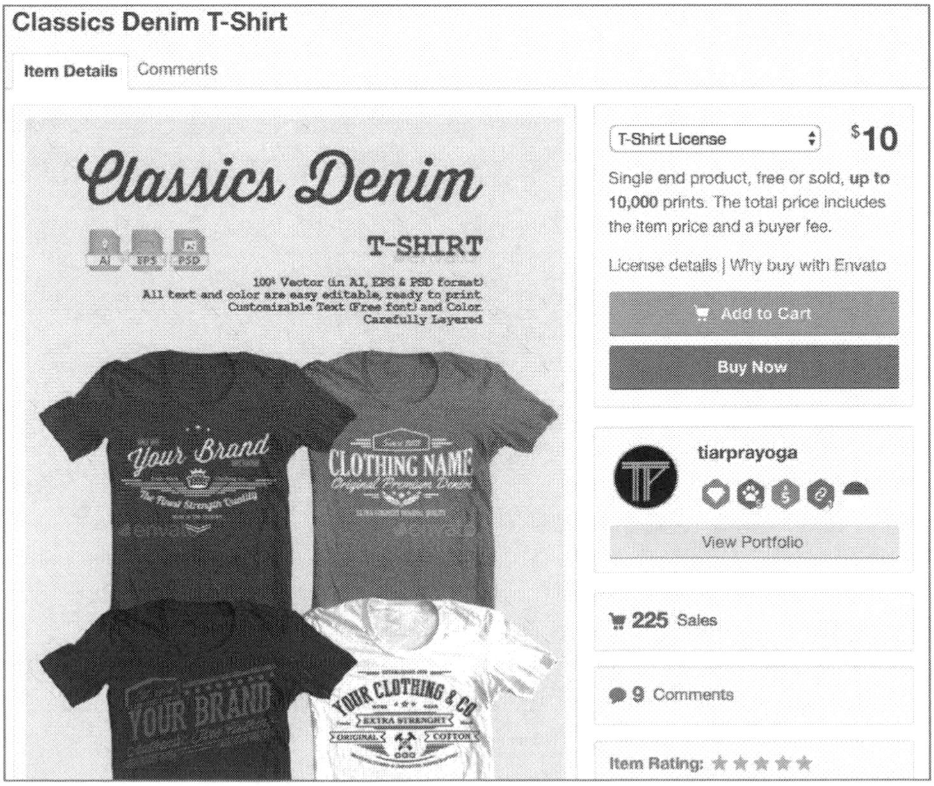

SpoonGraphics - blog.spoongraphics.co.uk

11 – YouTube Channels

Brad Colbow – iPad Design App Reviews
https://www.youtube.com/user/thebradcolbow

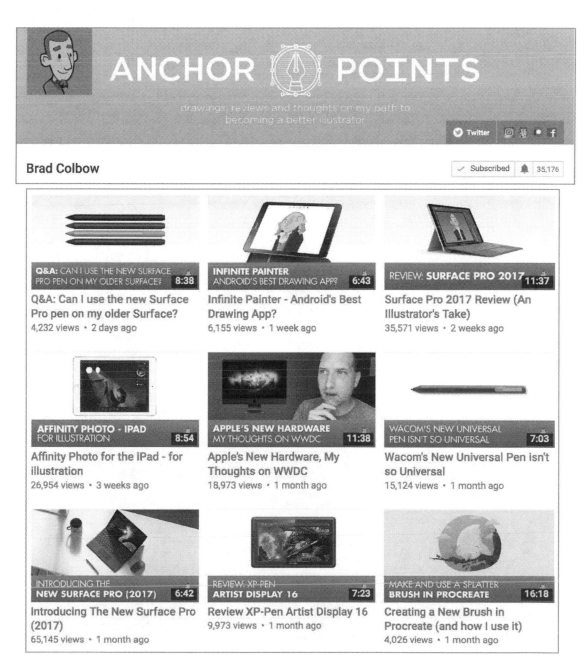

Sketchy Trav
https://www.youtube.com/user/SketchyTrav

Sketchy Trav

✓ Subscribed 🔔 61,625

Iron Fist VS Iron Man Drawing
2,496 views · 2 months ago

Drawing My Wife From Memory
5,711 views · 3 months ago

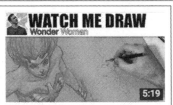

Watch Me Draw Wonder Woman
2,528 views · 3 months ago

Painting Characters with Watercolors
4,176 views · 5 months ago

Drawing a Superman Comic Book Cover
4,209 views · 5 months ago

Art Supply Subscription Box Review (Sketch Box)
10,088 views · 6 months ago

Monster Character Concepts
3,587 views · 7 months ago

Inktober Sketchbook Tour
6,009 views · 7 months ago

Sketch Book Tour! I'm Back!
5,988 views · 8 months ago

Disney Princesses and Mashups Sketchbook Update
15,448 views · 11 months ago

How To Draw Hands
17,485 views · 11 months ago

Going Through My Wife's Sketch Book
35,175 views · 11 months ago

Mike Henry – Procreate demos
https://www.youtube.com/user/zatransis

Mike Henry

✓ Subscribed 🔔 18,321

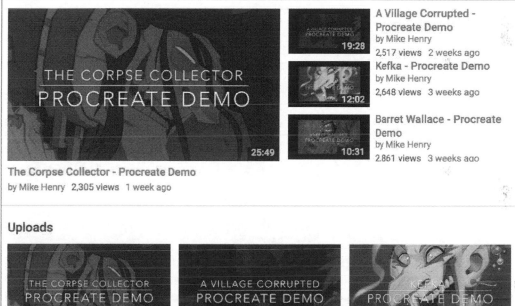

A Village Corrupted - Procreate Demo
by Mike Henry
2,517 views 2 weeks ago

Kefka - Procreate Demo
by Mike Henry
2,648 views 3 weeks ago

Barret Wallace - Procreate Demo
by Mike Henry
2,861 views 3 weeks ago

The Corpse Collector - Procreate Demo
by Mike Henry 2,305 views 1 week ago

Uploads

The Corpse Collector - Procreate Demo
2,305 views · 1 week ago

A Village Corrupted - Procreate Demo
2,517 views · 2 weeks ago

Kefka - Procreate Demo
2,648 views · 3 weeks ago

Popular uploads

Grigori - Procreate Demo (Character Design Exercise)
65,764 views · 9 months ago

The Barbed Monk - Procreate Demo
48,620 views · 11 months ago

Techniques Part 4 - Procreate Demo
43,831 views · 7 months ago

Draw With Jazza
https://www.youtube.com/user/DrawWithJazza

Draw with Jazza

Subscribe 1,666,148

JAZZA DRAWS LIVE - FAN Driven
ART CHALLENGE!
110,471 views • 1 day ago

"ARTY OUTFIT" - July 2017
Challenge of the Month!
156,239 views • 2 days ago

"STYLE SWAP" June COTM -
SHOWCASE and WINNERS!
206,118 views • 6 days ago

LIQUID PAPER ART CHALLENGE!
- Can you make Art with   ...
956,087 views • 1 week ago

UPDATE: Shirts, (Aussie) Con
Meetups + GIVEAWAYS!
77,265 views • 1 week ago

Let's Play: PASSPARTOUT - Can
the Artist WIN? (Pt.2)
664,435 views • 1 week ago

SMASH or PASS - FULL BODY
EDITION! - Random Character
575,980 views • 2 weeks ago

KFC Role Reversal Gets DARK -
Character Design Session!
443,350 views • 2 weeks ago

An ARTIST Plays PASSPARTOUT:
The Starving Artist Simulator!
838,258 views • 3 weeks ago

SHREK + RYUK - Character
MASHUP ART CHALLENGE!
314,558 views • 3 weeks ago

WORKING on my WEAKNESS:
Developing my Environment Art!
393,661 views • 4 weeks ago

"STYLE SWAP" - June 2017
Challenge of the Month!
362,127 views • 1 month ago

152

Seb Lester
https://www.youtube.com/user/Scomma

Seb Lester

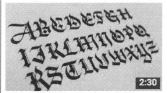

A-Z Blackletter Alphabet | Seb Lester Calligraphy
3,137 views • 3 days ago

New Calligraphy Compilation | Seb Lester
2,920 views • 5 days ago

Calligraphy for an amazing musician | Seb Lester Calligraphy
3,289 views • 1 week ago

Epic Doodle - Portal to another dimension - Plus I have a...
5,421 views • 1 month ago

'In my beginning' - T.S. Eliot | Seb Lester Calligraphy
6,837 views • 2 months ago

Boobies | Seb Lester Calligraphy
15,386 views • 5 months ago

Individuality | Seb Lester Calligraphy
7,687 views • 6 months ago

Carpe Diem (Seize the Day) | Seb Lester Calligraphy
5,395 views • 6 months ago

The Sun In Splendour | Seb Lester Calligraphy
8,709 views • 6 months ago

Tattoo Doodle (Tattoodle) | Seb Lester Calligraphy
5,929 views • 6 months ago

Believe | Seb Lester
7,095 views • 6 months ago

Art | Seb Lester Calligraphy
8,382 views • 7 months ago

Owen Video
youtube.com/user/simplebusinessvideo

Best Budget Vlogging Set Up for Starting a Business Vlog on...
118 views • 4 hours ago

Facebook Posting Tips to grow your YouTube Channel - YouTub...
531 views • 2 days ago

How to advertise your YouTube Channel - 5 Tips for using...
354 views • 4 days ago

Live Streaming Video Equipment Checklist (with bloopers!)
240 views • 1 week ago

Top 3 Small YouTuber Mistakes and how to avoid them NOW!
550 views • 1 week ago

7 Kickstarter Video Success Tips to get Your Project funded w/...
241 views • 1 week ago

How to get your first 1000 subscribers on YouTube
893 views • 2 weeks ago

How to have success with your YouTube Channel (with Nick...
415 views • 2 weeks ago

YouTube Tag Optimization (5 step process)
536 views • 3 weeks ago

12 - Free Images & Vectors

Pixabay - pixabay.com

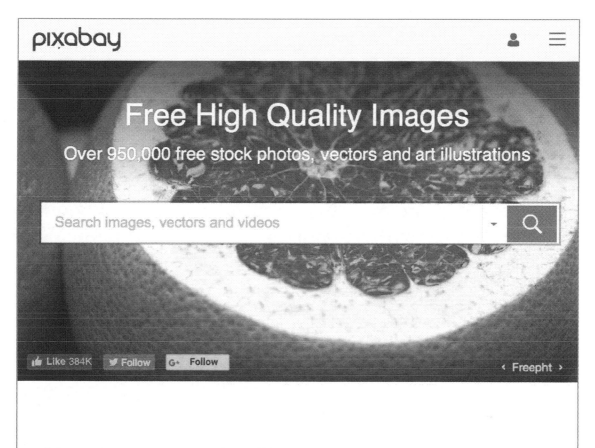

pixabay.com/en/service/faq

What is Pixabay?

On Pixabay you may find and share images free of copyrights. All pictures are released under Creative Commons CC0 into the public domain.

Can I use your images?

You can copy, modify, distribute, and use the images, even for commercial purposes, all without asking for permission or giving credits to the artist. However, depicted content may still be protected by trademarks, publicity or privacy rights. Read more in our blog.

pixabay.com/en/service/terms/#usage

Using Images and Videos

Images and Videos on Pixabay are released under Creative Commons CC0. To the extent possible under law, uploaders of Pixabay have waived their copyright and related or neighboring rights to these Images and Videos. You are free to adapt and use them for commercial purposes without attributing the original author or source. Although not required, a link back to Pixabay is appreciated.

Unsplash - unsplash.com

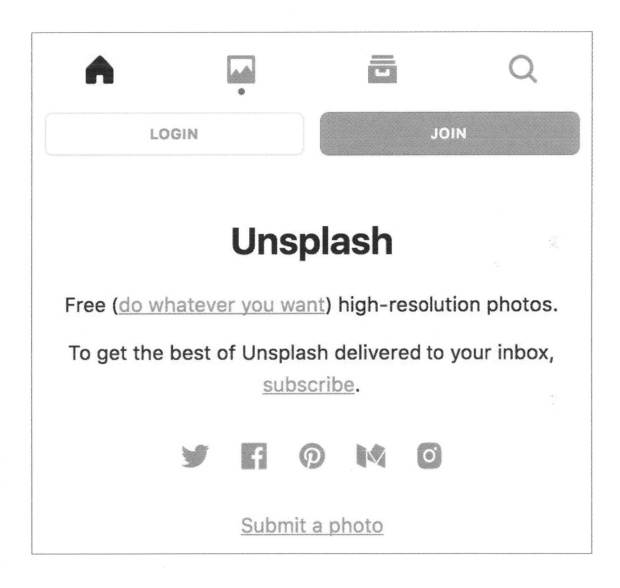

unsplash.com/license

License

All photos published on Unsplash are licensed under Creative Commons Zero which means you can copy, modify, distribute and use the photos for free, including commercial purposes, without asking permission from or providing attribution to the photographer or Unsplash.

For examples, check out Made with Unsplash.

madewith.unsplash.com

Questions? Read our FAQ.

community.unsplash.com/help

123RF - 123rf.com

Over 81 Million Stock Images, Vectors, Footage and Audio
Clips At Stunningly Low Prices

Photos

Vectors

Icons

Infographic

FreePik

freepik.com

Freepik is the leading search engine of free vector designs. Join the largest community of graphic designers in the world!

Freepik offers users, high quality graphic designs: exclusive illustrations and graphic resources carefully selected by our design team in order to provide our users with great content that can be used in both personal and commercial projects.

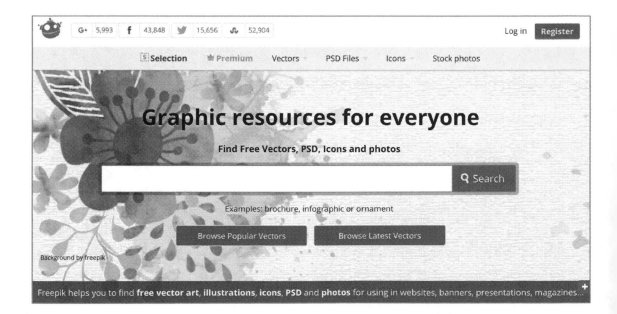

How can I use Freepik's resources for commercial purposes?

http://support.freepik.com/hc/en-us/articles/208978605-
How-can-I-use-Freepik-s-resources-for-commercial-
purposes-

In this guide we will explain the different ways you can use our resources applied to commercial use. Please remember to check our **Terms of Use** to ensure that you are using our images correctly complying these terms which are **applied for Premium and Free users** equally.

Can I use Freepik's resources on printed products aimed to sell?

If you desire to use our resources for this commercial purposes you must make sure that our resources are **not the principal element** of the designs that you are willing to include on your products.

This means that you must add other third party designs or self made images to create the composition of the design and **use our images as backgrounds or secondary elements** on this composition.

NO; NOT OK

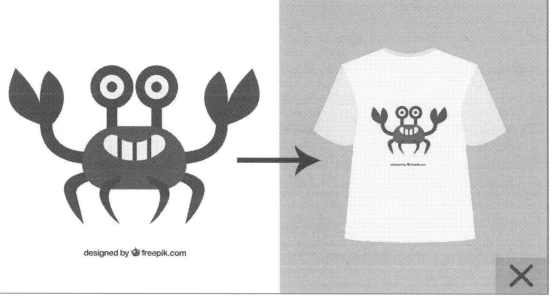

YES; OK

30 free public domain image websites (use with care)

99designs.com/blog/resources/public-domain-image-resources *by Rebecca Creger*

Free public domain images are an important cultural resource for everyone. But when using them as a designer you must be *extremely* vigilant about double-checking the license and terms of each of your desired images.

Some of these free public domain image websites will take time to look through and research properly, but there are a lot of amazing images in them that are worth finding. Just remember to keep these things in mind when sourcing images:

1. Does the license of the image allow you to use/distribute it in the way that you intend?
2. Is the quality of this image suitable for both print and web uses?
3. Are these images defined as public domain by images by the copyright laws of both countries that my client and I are citizens of?
4. Have I double-checked that this image is truly in the public domain? (run it through a search engine before using it.)
5. Does this image include trademarks, products, property, works of art, or people? If so make sure that a release has been obtained or that you obtain one yourself.

1. commons.wikimedia.org/wiki/Main_page

2. unsplash.com

3. flickr.com/commons

4. publicdomainpictures.net

5. magdeleine.co/license/cc0

6. oldbookillustrations.com

7. isorepublic.com

8. publicdomainvectors.org

9. 1millionfreepictures.com

10. freestockphotos.biz

11. jaymantri.com

12. realisticshots.com

13. startupstockphotos.com

14. flickr.com/photos/britishlibrary

15. publicdomainreview.org

16. viiintage.wpengine.com/public-domain-images

17. publicdomainarchive.com

18. jeshoots.com

19. designerspics.com

20. pixabay.com

21. everystockphoto.com

22. negativespace.co

23. deathtothestockphoto.com

24. flickr.com/photos/spacex

25. foodiesfeed.com

26. fancycrave.com

27. thepicpac.com

28. creativevix.com/index

29. barnimages.com

30. snapwiresnaps.tumblr.com

13 - Hiring Designers

Upwork - Upwork.com

Easily find quality freelancers

On Upwork you'll find a range of top talent, from programmers to designers, writers, customer support reps, and more.

- **Start by posting a job.** Tell us about your project and the specific skills required.

- **Upwork analyzes your needs.** Our search functionality uses data science to highlight freelancers based on their skills, helping you find talent that's a good match.

- **We send you a shortlist of likely candidates.** You can also search our site for talent, and freelancers can view your job and submit proposals too.

Work with someone perfect for your team

WEB DEVELOPERS	MOBILE DEVELOPERS	DESIGNERS & CREATIVES	WRITERS
VIRTUAL ASSISTANTS	CUSTOMER SERVICE AGENTS	SALES & MARKETING EXPERTS	ACCOUNTANTS & CONSULTANTS

HOW IT WORKS

FIND

Post a job to tell us about your project. We'll quickly match you with the right freelancers.

HIRE

Browse profiles, reviews, and proposals then interview top candidates. Hire a favorite and begin your project.

WORK

Use the Upwork platform to chat, share files, and collaborate from your desktop or on the go.

PAY

Invoicing and payments happen through Upwork. With Upwork Protection, only pay for work you authorize.

168

Shirt Design Freelancers

Zivan B.
T-Shirts EXPERT Graphic Designer

$50.00 / hr $40k+ earned   99% Job Succ   ⊙ Serbia

I create T-shirts that people love to wear. I guarantee you: 1.
Unlimited revisions 2. You'll love my work TESTIMONIALS FROM MY
PREVIOUS UPWORK CLIENTS: "Ver ...

| T-Shirt Design | Logo Design | CorelDRAW ✓ |

| Adobe Photoshop | 6 more |

Tests: Portfolios:
15   25

D. D.
Expert Graphic Designer | T-shirt | T-shirt QUOTES researchs

$63.00 / hr $10k+ earned   95% Job Succ   ⊙ Indonesia

I'm an artist based in Indonesia. I have over 4 years of experience in
Tshirt designs, teespring, spreadshirt, redbubble and many more!! I
have a strong inter ...

| Adobe Photoshop ✓ | CorelDRAW ✓ | Adobe Illustrator ✓ |

| English | 1 more |

Tests: Portfolios:
10   18

Victor S.
T-Shirt Designer & Illustrator

$30.00 / hr $6k+ earned   98% Job Succ   ⊙ Mexico

Hi, I'm Victor, a Top Rated creative professional with 10+ years in the
field, I design t-shirts most of of the time though, my skills set is
quite wide and it ...

| T-Shirt Design | Adobe Illustrator | Adobe Photoshop |

| WordPress | 3 more |

Test: 1   Portfolios:
            49

Vasilije S.
T-shirt Designer / Vector Illustrator

$34.00 / hr $10k+ earned   94% Job Succ   ⊙ Serbia

Greetings, I have been working at Upwork full-time (More than 2
years). Motivated graphic designer with 10+ years experience. I'm
highly experienced in Ado ...

| Adobe Photoshop ✓ | Adobe Illustrator ✓ | T-Shirt Design |

| Illustration | 4 more |

Tests: 4   Portfolios:
            38

Fiverr - Fiverr.com

Fiverr is a site where graphic designers and artists can offer services. You can search for those who offer to make shirt designs

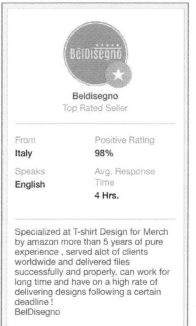

Beldisegno
Top Rated Seller

From	Positive Rating
Italy	**98%**
Speaks	Avg. Response Time
English	**4 Hrs.**

Specialized at T-shirt Design for Merch by amazon more than 5 years of pure experience , served alot of clients worldwide and delivered files successfully and properly, can work for long time and have on a high rate of delivering designs following a certain deadline !
BelDisegno

Read more

You can view someone's Fiverr Profile in order to see their location, rating, languages spoken, and average response time.

You can also choose to only search for Top Rated Sellers on Fiverr.

Compare Packages

	$10 Basic	$20 Standard	$50 Premium
Description	**TEXT BASED DESIGNS** I SHALL DESIGN CLEAN, EDGY & SIMPLE TYPOGRAPHY BASED DESIGN UP TO 3 COLORS	**PREMIUM PACK** ALL FEATURES OF BASIC PACKAGE ALONG WITH VINTAGE EFFECT, PREMIUM TYPOGRAPHY & GRAPHIC ILLUSTRATION	**Bulk PACK** 10 Designs TYPOGRAPHY & Basic Graphic ILLUSTRATION *Highly recommended to contact me before order
Commercial Use	✔	✔	✔
High Resolution	✔	✔	✔
Enhanced Detailing	–	✔	–
Revisions	2	2	2
Delivery time	⦿ 3 days ○ 1 day (+$5)	⦿ 3 days ○ 1 day (+$5)	⦿ 4 days ○ 1 day (+$10)
	Select $10	Select $20	Select $50

Fiverr designers can also offer packages and add-ons with different delivery times and other features.

FIVERR PRO - fiverr.com/introducing-pro

This is a BIG step for Fiverr!

Connecting world-class talent with professional business buyers, for endless possibilities. Hand-vetted. High-end. On-demand.

Look for the Fiverr Pro logo!

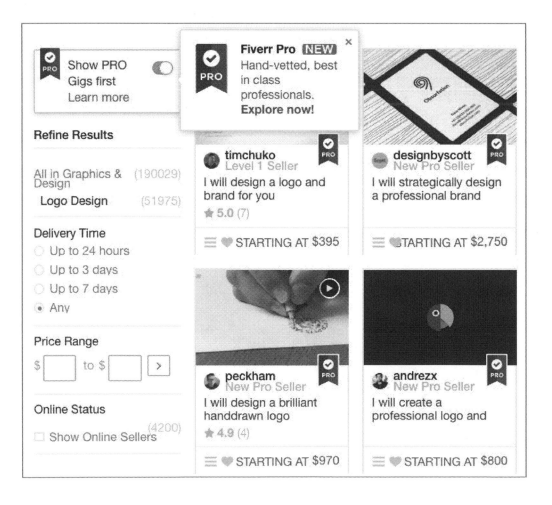

Get more, Do more:

High Quality Environment

We hand-pick the talent labeled as Pro, so you can be sure you're surrounding yourself with the very best out there.

Hassle-free Process

We're expanding the same simple and efficient Fiverr ordering system, that allows you to focus on what you do best.

VIP Experience

We're here, with dedicated Pro Customer Support and Success Managers, to make sure every project is a successful one.

Trustworthy Collaborations

We're committed to making you feel safe, with secure communications and transactions.

PeoplePerHour - PeoplePerHour.com

How it works:

peopleperhour.com/static/how-it-works-buyer

1. Three simple ways to get started!
   - **Browse Hourlies™: fixed price offers ready to start immediately**
   - **Post a Job - let people find you!**
   - **Search profiles and contact freelancers directly**

2. Manage, Pay & Communicate all in one place: your WorkStream™

3. Rate the Seller and keep it rolling!

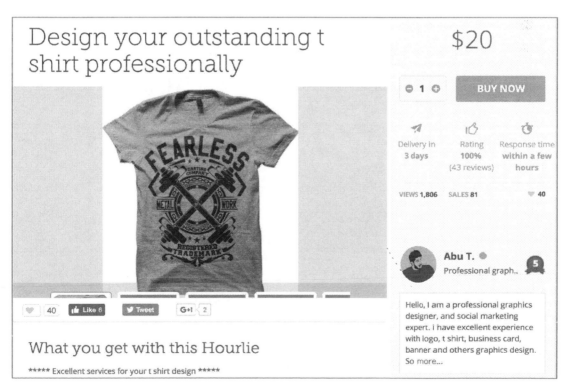

OnlineJobs - onlinejobs.ph

World's largest and safest marketplace for finding rock star Filipino workers.

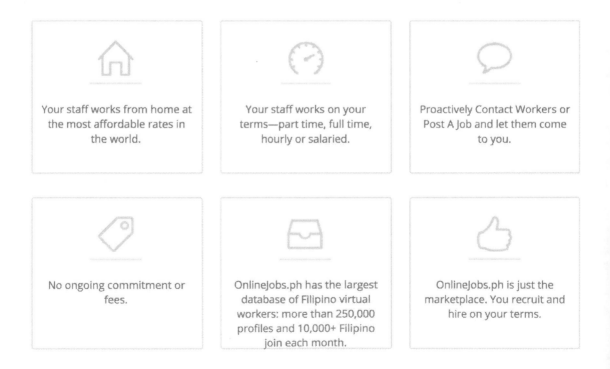

Your staff works from home at the most affordable rates in the world.

Your staff works on your terms—part time, full time, hourly or salaried.

Proactively Contact Workers or Post A Job and let them come to you.

No ongoing commitment or fees.

OnlineJobs.ph has the largest database of Filipino virtual workers: more than 250,000 profiles and 10,000+ Filipino join each month.

OnlineJobs.ph is just the marketplace. You recruit and hire on your terms.

Why look to the Philippines?

You'll find countless options as you search for virtual help to support your business. But basic cultural traits, advanced education, and proficient English make Filipinos the ideal virtual workers. After years of experience, we've found they can't be beat.

We remove the middleman

We don't mark-up salaries. We provide you a simple place to find and contact quality workers. Then you hire them as you see fit.

Behance - Behance.net

What is Behance?

Mission Statement:

Behance, part of the Adobe family, is the leading online platform to showcase & discover creative work. The creative world updates their work in one place to broadcast it widely and efficiently. Companies explore the work and access talent on a global scale.

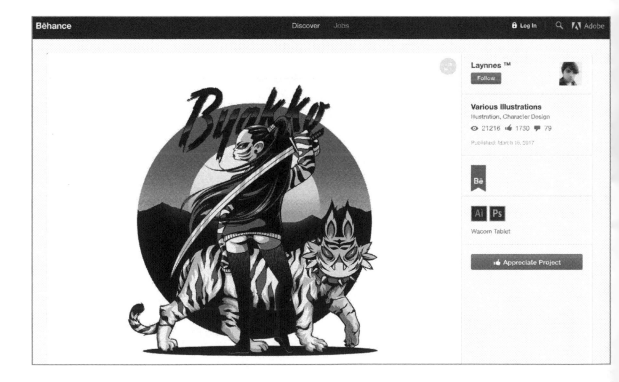

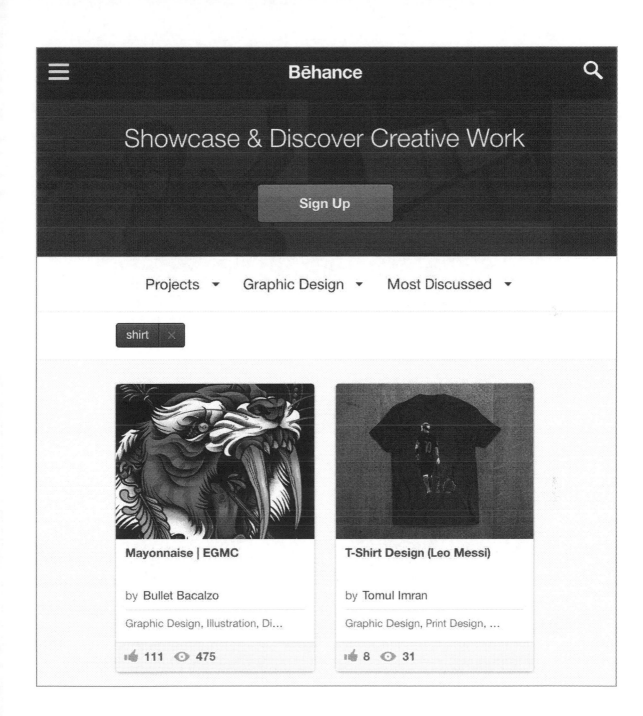

Freelancer - freelancer.com

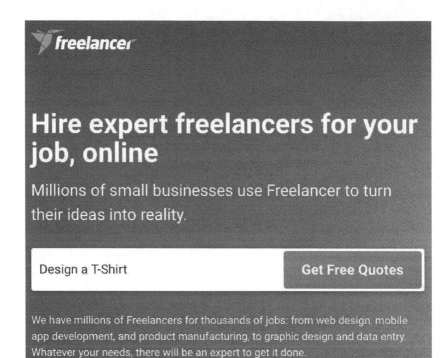

freelancer

Hire expert freelancers for your job, online

Millions of small businesses use Freelancer to turn their ideas into reality.

| Design a T-Shirt | Get Free Quotes |

We have millions of Freelancers for thousands of jobs: from web design, mobile app development, and product manufacturing, to graphic design and data entry. Whatever your needs, there will be an expert to get it done.

Let's select a job type:

Based on your job **"Design a T-Shirt"** we recommend **Posting a Contest**.

Project
Receive competitive bids from talented freelancers to work on your job.

○

Contest
Freelancers submit work for you to review before you award a winner.

◉

Guru - guru.com

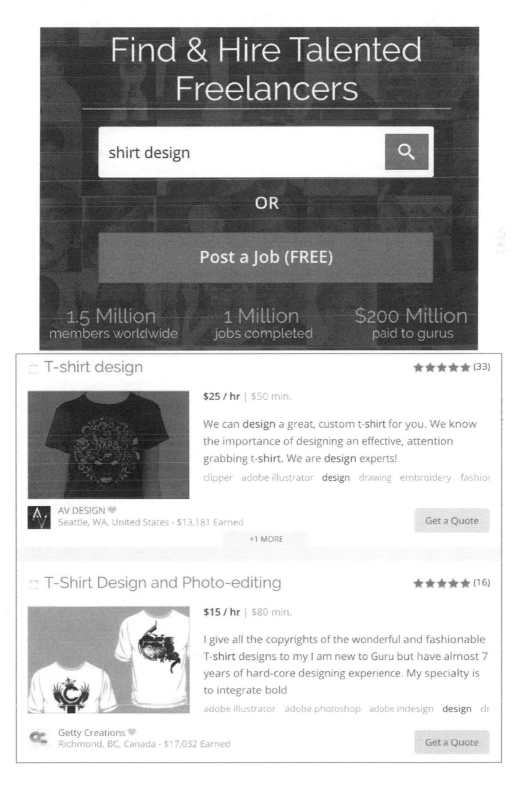

TaskRabbit - taskrabbit.com

TaskRabbit

1. Fill Out Task Details   2. View Taskers & Prices   3. Confirm & Book

Trust & Safety Guarantee:
$1MM insurance guarantee on every task.

Graphic Design Change

YOUR TASK LOCATION

☑ Is this a virtual task?

Enter street address | Unit or Apt #

Many people think of TaskRabbit for local, in-person jobs, but they also allow for virtual tasks in graphic designs as you can see above.

99designs - 99designs.com/projects

Dribble - dribbble.com/designers

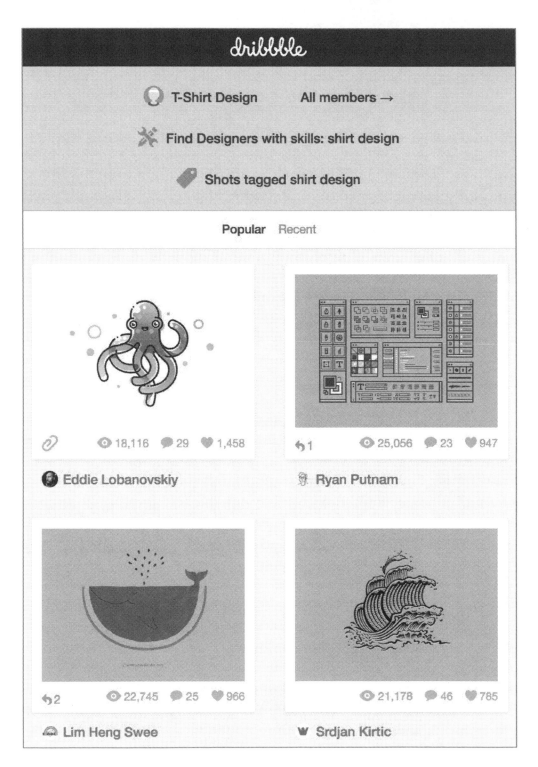

DesignCrowd - designcrowd.com

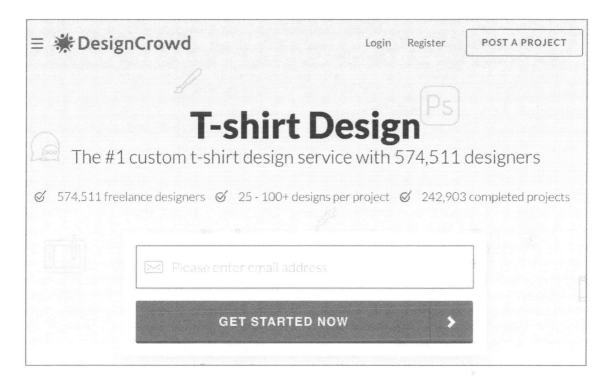

WorkMarket - workmarket.com

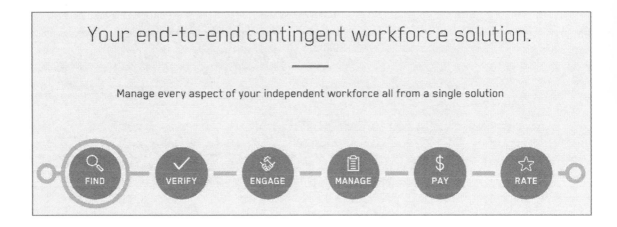

Toptal - toptal.com

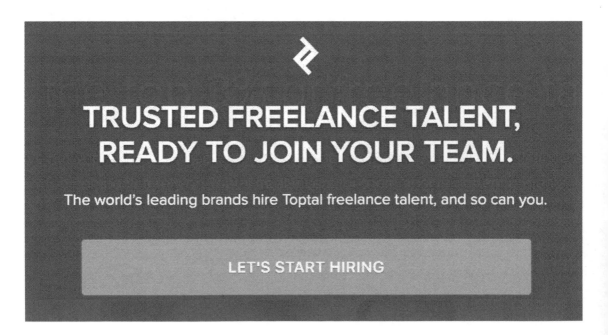

14 - Shirt Mockups

Make-merch.com Mockups
Lifestyle T-Pics

Lifestyle Tee Picks

Create Your Design and Click DOWNLOAD IMAGE
(for registered users only)

Use this page to create unique lifestyle pics.

Lifestyle pics sell more!

Upload your design, create a lifestyle pic and
download it so you can promote your designs on
social media.

Registered users can download these images
without the make-merch watermark.

Select Fit Type:

T-Shirt Color (for viewing only, not included in design):

Select Lifestyle Background Image:

Add Filter to Lifestylebackground:

Select Emoji:

Line 1:

| I'm on twitter | Bangers |

Select Font Color Line 1:

SAVE DESIGN LINK TO CLIPBOARD

DOWNLOAD IMAGE

188

Make your own great-looking images like this one using the Make-Merch mockup generator!

PlaceIt - placeit.net

PlaceIt.net has some AMAZING image and video mockups. They have then for both images as well as for videos.

To see the t-shirt options, be sure to click on the Apparel & Print link at the top of their website.

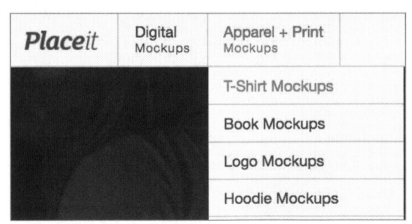

Here are some examples from the IMAGES section of PlaceIt.

placeit.net/c/apparel/?f_devices=T-Shirt

In the menu on the left hand side, you can choose VIDEO to see the available video options for PlaceIt mockups.

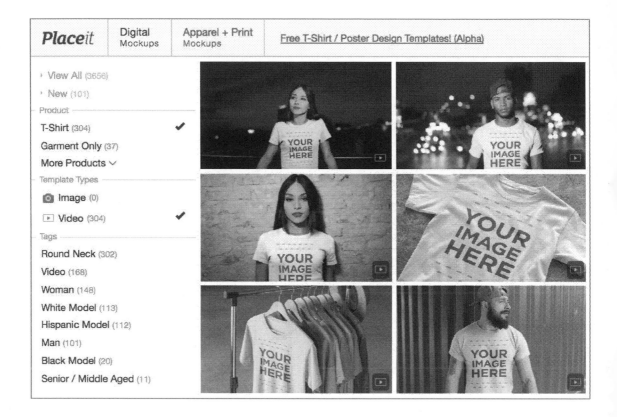

placeit.net/c/apparel/?f_types=video&f_devices=T-Shirt

This link with get you a 15% discount from PlaceIt.net:
placeit.refersion.com/c/d744c

QUIK – quik.gopro.com

Quik is an amazing (and free) app for both iOS and Android that lets you create short, amazing looking videos for social media or other online promotion from simple images (like shirt designs or mockups).

The only requirement is that you use at least FIVE images to make a video. You can download your shirt images from Amazon's product pages or use your own Merch By Amazon design files.

iOS app:
https://itunes.apple.com/us/app/quik-gopro-video-editor-to-edit-clips-with-music/id694164275?mt=8

Android app:
https://play.google.com/store/apps/details?id=com.stupeflix.replay&hl=en

Viddyoze – MerchVideos.com

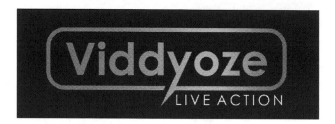

Create Jaw-Dropping LIVE ACTION Video Animations In Just 3 Clicks

Yesterday, You Would Have Needed A Film Crew, Actors, And Thousands Of Dollars. Today, You Just Need Viddyoze Live Action.

> **Posts**
>
> **Chris Green**
> Published by Chris Green [?] · 2 mins · 🌐
>
> Show off your super powers with this great shirt available from Amazon!
>
> https://www.amazon.com/dp/B01AUA6EE0
>
> **Boost Post**
>
> 6 Views
>
> 👍 Like   💬 Comment   ↗ Share

ShirtMockup

http://shirtmockup.com

ShirtMockup is a free tool to realistically mockup your designs on tees.

Upload your art. Mock it up. Download your image for FREE!

ShirtMockup PRO

http://www.shirtmockup.com/amember/signup.php

Why go PRO?

Features	Pro	Basic
Faster than Photoshop	⊛	⊛
Photorealistic Results	⊛	⊛
Unlimited Garment Colors	⊛	⊛
Rotate / Scale Sliders	⊛	
Large Mockup Images	⊛	
Watermark-free Images	⊛	
Updated with New Templates	⊛	
Opacity Control / Reset Buttons	⊛	
Upload Images over 300k	⊛	
Template Variations		
Front	⊛	⊛
Back	⊛	
Fitted (ghosted)	⊛	⊛
Flat (loose)	⊛	⊛
Flat (ironed)	⊛	

Why go PRO?

Garment Styles	Pro	Basic
Standard T-Shirt	✪	✪
Distressed T-Shirt	✪	✪
Ladies T-Shirt	✪	
Zip-up Hoodie	✪	
V-Neck T-Shirt	✪	
Pullover Hoodie	✪	
Ringer T-Shirt	✪	
Ladies Tank Tops	✪	
Men's Long Sleeve	✪	
Tri-blend T-Shirt	✪	
Polo T-Shirt	✪	
Men's Thermals	✪	
Baggy Tees	✪	

ShirtMockup Pro subscribers get unlimited access to our Pro template library with bigger, watermark-free mockups. Still blazingly fast!

ARSENAL

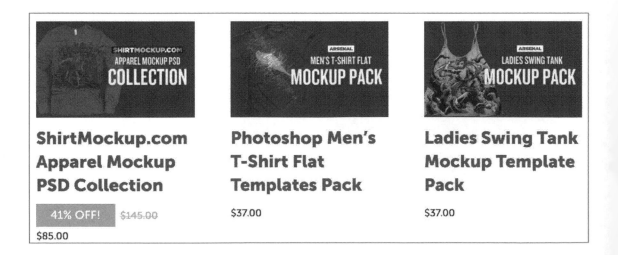

go media™

ARSENAL

PROFESSIONAL DESIGN WEAPONRY

https://arsenal.gomedia.us?raf=ref3264379

Mockup Templates

Everything looks better in the real-world right? Of course it does. Use these Photoshop mockup templates to make your design look like it has been printed on a real t-shirt, beanie, sticker, billboard, hoodie, iPad, iPhone, notebook, tank top, polo, album cover, cd, poster, etc. It makes it that much easier to sell your design to your client, customer, or friends. Don't be surprised when people say, "Woah, I want that!"

ShirtMockup.com Apparel Mockup PSD Collection

41% OFF! ~~$145.00~~

$85.00

Photoshop Men's T-Shirt Flat Templates Pack

$37.00

Ladies Swing Tank Mockup Template Pack

$37.00

Creative Market – creativemarket.com

Creative Market has some awesome mockup options. Simply search their site for 'mockup shirt' and you'll have plenty to choose from.

creativemarket.com/search/mockup/shirt

Here is an example of a t-shirt mockup service offered on Creative Market. Be sure to carefully read the licensing agreement and terms before purchasing to be sure that you can use the images the way you intend to.

creativemarket.com/tompe/51207-Unique-T-Shirt-mock-up

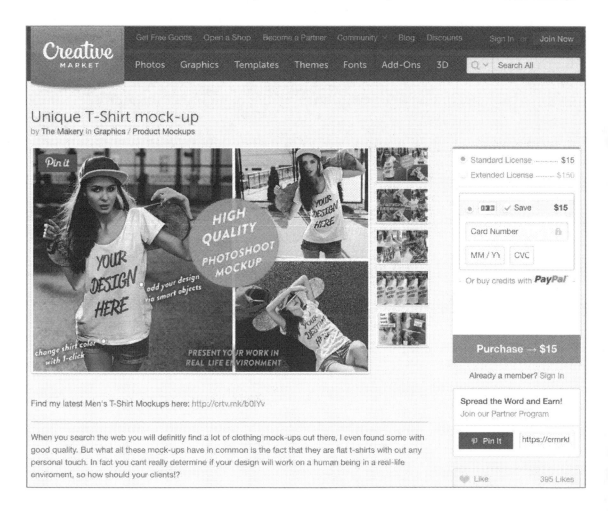

15 - Additional Resources

MerchTools - Merchtools.com

Handy Tools For Merch by Amazon Sellers

Handy collection of Merch by amazon shortcuts and automated market research tools: researching niche keywords and studying the market never been so convenient.

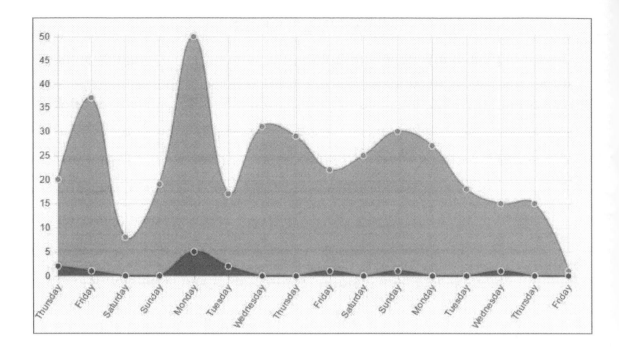

-Notifications on new sales, cancellations and Merch Account Logout.

-QuickEditor for fast editing with search.

-Shows Days Left Before Deletion.

-Lists All your ASINs so you can import them to your store (Shopify / woocommerce).

-Sales Chart For the Past 14 days. -Monthly growth charts. -Today's Sales with quick edit.

-Support Group.

Merch Reports – MerchReports.com

Merch Reports gives Merch By Amazon sellers unprecedented access to detailed analytics of their sales! Upload your Merch By Amazon sales reports to see a comprehensive breakdown of your sales including SIZE and COLOR breakdown!

Merch Reports runs locally on YOUR COMPUTER! Your sales and data are never shared online. Keep control of your data and your designs confidential with Merch Reports.

Payoneer – Payoneer.com

Payoneer allows ***international designers*** to use the Merch By Amazon platform.

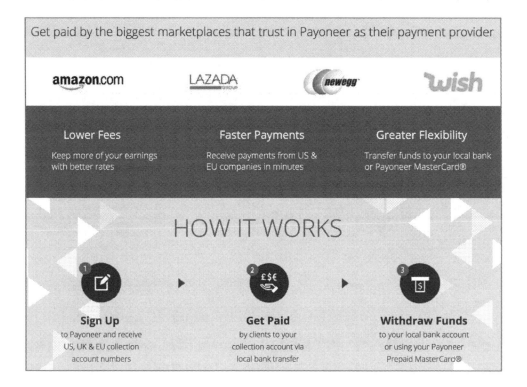

Payoneer & Amazon - payoneer.com/en/amazon

Amazon & Payoneer -

amazon.com/gp/help/customer/display.html?nodeId=201990250

Merchoneer – Merchoneer.com

Sign up for Payoneer using the link
Merchoneer.com to earn $75!

Papaly – papaly.com

Papaly is an awesome FREE site/Chrome extension that you can use to organize bookmarks and keep track of sites and searches.

merchbookmarks.com is a Papaly site.

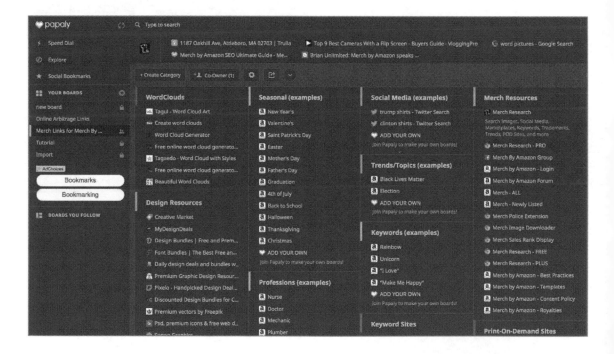

Use it as inspiration to make your own. You can have a public or private Papaly page. You can also share it by invitation only.

16 - Keyword Sites

merchinformer.com/keyword-tools

keyword.io

thesaurus.com

yoast.com

merchinformer.com/keyword-tools

kwfinder.com

synonym.com

moz.com/explorer

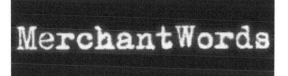

merchantwords.com

keywordtooldominator.com

wordstream.com

keywordtool.io

adwords.google.com/keywordplanner

ılıl• SERPs

serps.com/tools/keyword-research

answerthepublic.com

app.scientificseller.com

ubersuggest.io

oodle suggest

oodlesuggest.com

17 - Trademark Sites

USPTO - uspto.gov

United States Patent and Trademark Office

Search trademark database

Search database for trademark registrations and applications by mark, owner, or serial/registration number with Trademark Electronic Search System (TESS).

Select A Search Option

▶ **Basic Word Mark Search (New User)**
This option cannot be used to search design marks.

▶ **Word and/or Design Mark Search (Structured)**
This option is used to search word and/or design marks. **NOTE:** You must first use the **Design Search Code Manual** to look up the relevant Design Codes.

▶ **Word and/or Design Mark Search (Free Form)**
This option allows you to construct word and/or design searches using Boolean logic and multiple search fields. **NOTE:** You must first use the **Design Search Code Manual** to look up the relevant Design Codes.

United States Patent and Trademark Office
Home | Site Index | Search | FAQ | Glossary | Guides | Contacts | eBusiness | eBiz alerts | News | Help

Trademarks > Trademark Electronic Search System (TESS)

TESS was last updated on Tue May 23 03:21:06 EDT 2017

| TESS HOME | STRUCTURED | FREE FORM | BROWSE DICT | SEARCH OG | BOTTOM | HELP |

WARNING: AFTER **SEARCHING** THE USPTO DATABASE, EVEN IF **YOU** THINK THE RESULTS ARE "O.K.," DO **NOT** ASSUME THAT YOUR MARK CAN BE REGISTERED AT THE USPTO. AFTER YOU FILE AN APPLICATION, THE USPTO MUST DO ITS OWN SEARCH AND OTHER REVIEW, AND MIGHT **REFUSE TO REGISTER** YOUR MARK.

View Search History: ▢

◉ Plural and Singular ◯ Singular

◉ Live and Dead ◯ Live ◯ Dead

Search Term: _____

Field: Combined Word Mark (BI,TI,MP,TL)

Result Must Contain: All Search Terms (AND)

[Submit Query] [Clear Query]

212

TMHunt – <u>TMHunt.com</u>

Checking TESS and evaluating its results may be confusing and even discouraging, especially for newbies. Searching for one query at a time is slow and boring in any case.

On TMHunt.com you'll find 3 different search types to avoid trademark infringement, avoid rejections and keep your Merch account safe. Results will show matching trademarks in IC 025 (clothing class) only and the database is updated daily with official USPTO records.

- Multi Search: Enter a list of quotes, slogans or keywords;

- Split Search: Enter one quote to split it and search for its individual parts. All combinations of adjacent words will be searched, from single words to the whole sentence. To explain it better, searching "YOU CAN'T SCARE ME I'M A BASEBALL MOM" on TESS won't show any results, but using the Split Search on TMHunt you'll find two "hidden" text trademarks ("YOU CAN'T SCARE" and "BASEBALL MOM"). Filter by "Status: Live" and "Type: Text" to hide design-only and dead trademarks.

- Wildcard Search: use an asterisk as a wildcard character, e.g. "IN * WE TRUST";

You can filter results by status (live or dead), type (text, design, typeset) and registration.

Merch users most likely want to avoid "Text" trademarks (Standard Character Marks) with a "live" status.

Clicking on the serial number will bring up the USPTO trademark page, where you can check further details.

In the "Reports" menu on top, you can browse clothing trademarks applications filed last week, registered last week and currently published for opposition.

Trademarkia - trademarkia.com

TRADEMARK STATEMENT OF USE

The Statement of Use is a sworn declaration that your trademark is currently in use in commerce in connection with all of the products and/or services listed in your trademark application.

Click here for details »

TRADEMARK WATCH

Trademark watch identifies verbal and graphical elements, phonetic similarities, local dialects that could be considered similar to your trademark and could present a risk to your trademark's value.

Click here for details »

TRADEMARK OFFICE ACTION

An Office Action is a letter issued by an Examiner for the United States Patent and Trademark Office. The letter will let you know if there is any conflicting trademarks that may prevent your Trademark Registration.

Click here for details »

TRADEMARK ASSIGNMENTS

The owner of a trademark may change for various reasons. Some trademark owners transfer their ownership of a mark to another entity, which is called an assignment

Click here for details »

TRADEMARK REVIVAL

Trademarkia makes it easy to revive your abandoned trademark application and retain rights in your established application.

Click here for details »

TRADEMARK RENEWAL (SECTION 8 OR SECTION 9)

You must renew your Trademark every 10-year; and You must show use of your trademark no later than the 6th-year after your mark is registered.

Click here for details »

18 - Merch Podcasts

Coming Soon!
merchpodcast.com

facebook.com/groups/merchpodcast

merchentrepreneur.com by Elaine Heney

Facebook Group:
facebook.com/groups/merchentrepreneurs

WITH GLEN AND YONG

merchminds.libsyn.com
Glen Zubia & Yong Jae Chong

Facebook Group:
facebook.com/groups/1824530797822546

19 - Merch Courses
Intro: Udemy.com/MerchByAmazonIntro

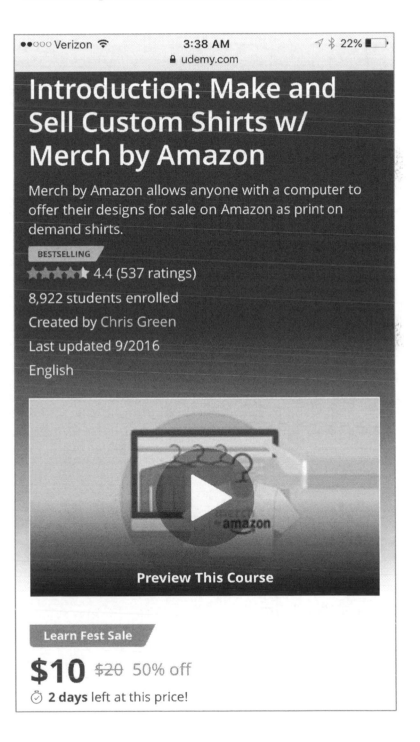

Advanced: Udemy.com/MerchByAmazon

●●○○○ Verizon 🛜   **3:38 AM**   ⌖ ✳ 22% ▮▭

🔒 udemy.com

Introduction: Make and Sell Custom Shirts w/ Merch by Amazon

Merch by Amazon allows anyone with a computer to offer their designs for sale on Amazon as print on demand shirts.

BESTSELLING

★★★★★ 4.4 (537 ratings)

8,922 students enrolled

Created by Chris Green

Last updated 9/2016

English

▶

Preview This Course

Learn Fest Sale

$10 ~~$20~~ 50% off

⏱ **2 days** left at this price!

Proven Merch Live – Merch.live

This was a small, personal event hosted in California with high-volume Merch By Amazon sellers sharing their best tips and secrets. There are replays available of the sessions at www.merch.live

Modules We Covered

Module 1: Understanding Merch By Amazon
Module 2: Signing Up and What to Expect
Module 3: Design – Ideas, Learning, and Hiring/Outsourcing
Module 4: Planting Your Money Trees
Module 5: Watering Your Money Trees
(Facebook Ads, AMS - Amazon Marketing Services)
Module 6: Licensing – Power of Partnerships
Module 7: Local Business Opportunities
Module 8: Future of Merch – Expanding Your Empire

Make and Sell Custom Shirts Using Merch by Amazon

Course Description

Merch by Amazon is Amazon's newest platform for content creators. It allows anyone to create and sell shirts right on Amazon's website with no upfront costs or minimum print runs. Anyone can now easily create custom branded shirts that their fans will love to wear. This course will help you get started and learn how to use the platform both optimally and creatively.

This course includes video demos of shirt designs in Adobe Photoshop as well as actual creation of an Amazon product page for a new shirt design. If you want to learn how to take advantage of this incredible new platform to not only create awesome shirts but to also make money along the way, then this course is for you.

What are the requirements?

- Students should have an Amazon account to take this course

- Students should be comfortable entering banking and tax information into their Amazon account

- Basic photo editing skills (Photoshop or Illustrator) are beneficial but not mandatory

What am I going to get from this course?

- Create a Merch by Amazon account

- Understand the digital file requirements for shirt designs

- Use the Merch by Amazon platform to create their own shirt designs available for sale on Amazon

- Become familiar with all of the Merch by Amazon account settings

- Forward and mask domains

- Create their own Amazon Associates account

Proven Merch Cource – ProvenMerch.com

Tutpad - tutpad.com

Tutpad offers users, high quality design tutorials carefully selected by their design team in order to provide their users a completely custom learning experience, Learn from experienced and professional instructors in design, photography, video and more.

CreativeLive - creativelive.com

CreativeLive has some great graphic design courses, including t-shirt design.

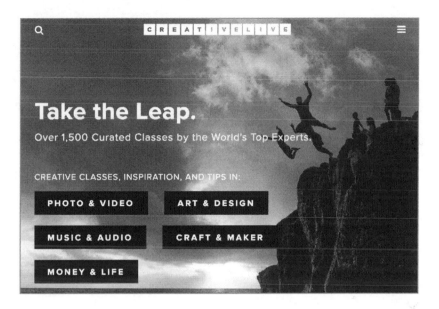

You can narrow down your search using search terms like 'shirt':

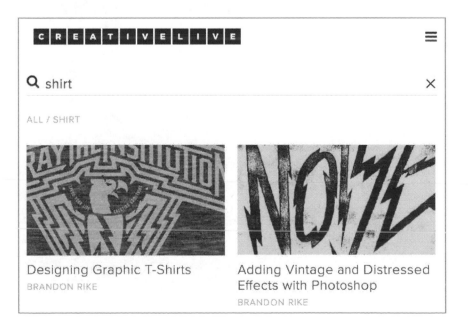

Skillshare – skillshare.com

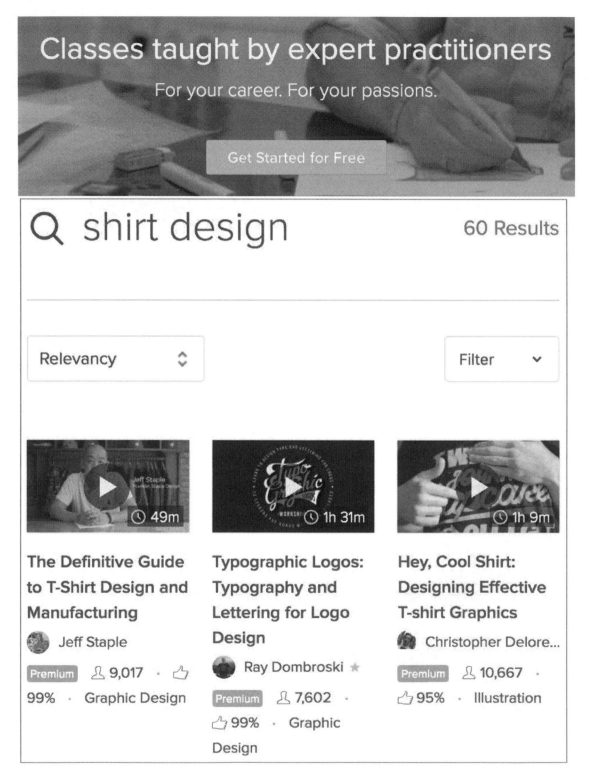

Classes taught by expert practitioners

For your career. For your passions.

Get Started for Free

Q **shirt design**   60 Results

Relevancy ⇕   Filter ⌄

⏱ 49m   ⏱ 1h 31m   ⏱ 1h 9m

The Definitive Guide to T-Shirt Design and Manufacturing

Jeff Staple

Premium ⎍ 9,017 · 👍

99% · Graphic Design

Typographic Logos: Typography and Lettering for Logo Design

Ray Dombroski ✦

Premium ⎍ 7,602 ·

👍 99% · Graphic Design

Hey, Cool Shirt: Designing Effective T-shirt Graphics

Christopher Delore...

Premium ⎍ 10,667 ·

👍 95% · Illustration

Other Udemy courses – Udemy.com

There are lots of other courses on Udemy about Merch By Amazon and t-shirt design. Just search, check reviews, and get to work!

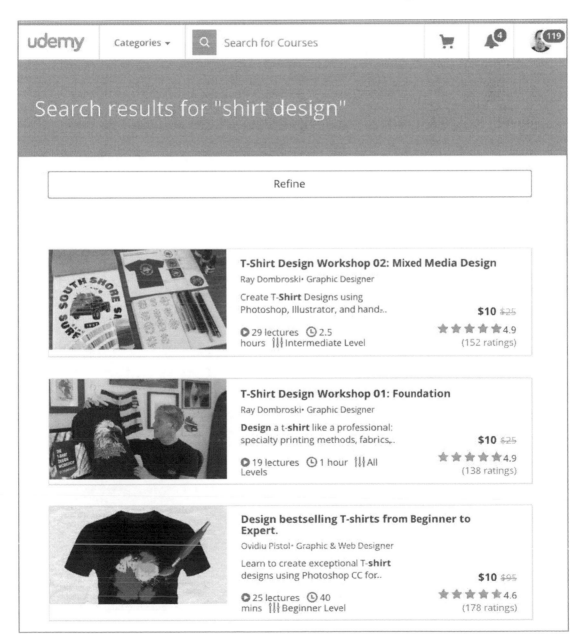

20 - Trackable Link Services

Sellio - sell.io

Sell.io let's you add TRACKING and ANALYTICS to your traffic BEFORE you send them to Amazon.com!

Sell.io is included FREE for members of The RiverBank! http://River-Bank.com

You can add the **Facebook Tracking Pixel** to your traffic using sell.io.

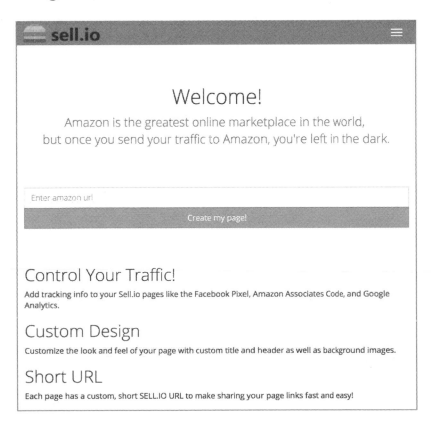

sell.io

Update new landing page

Product info
Your product url | Required

> https://amazon.com/dp/B0167L3TKS/

SEO Title | Optional, let empty to parse value from page

> Amazon.com: I Love Koalas Shirt, I Heart Koalas: Clothing

SEO Description | Optional, let empty to parse value from page

> Buy I Love Koalas Shirt, I Heart Koalas and other T-Shirts at Amazon.com. Our wide select

Main image | Optional, let empty to parse value from page

> https://images-na.ssl-images-amazon.com/images/I/41Jp7g1eGNL._UX679_.jpg

Amazon Associates Code | Optional

> Enter your affiliate tag value

Amazon Seller Id | Optional, only for non merch products

> Enter your seller id value

Facebook pixel tracking
Your facebook code or id | Optional

>

☐ **Track add to cart via pixel**

Google analytics
Your analytics code or id | Optional

>

☐ **Track add to cart via analytics**

Background:
Upload your page background | Optional

>   📂 Browse ...

Select background position | Optional

Select background size | Optional

> Tile ⬍

Update my page!

Genius Link - Geni.us

https://geni.us/Lqz2yOB

This special referral link enables bonus features like the use of the MRCH.LY and MRCH.IT short URLs.

Dynamic Link Destinations

Improve conversions by marketing to your entire audience. Create a single link that routes every user to the right place based on their language, device, operating system, country and even date of click.

Targeted Marketing Audiences

Create remarketing pools using tracking pixels from Facebook, Twitter, Google Adwords and more to better track your audience. Create more effective marketing campaigns in the future based on who clicked today.

A/B Testing

Automatically route a percentage of your clicks to different destinations for the same audience segment. Compare landing page and storefront performance.

geniuslink

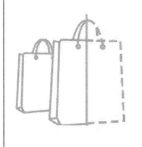

Automagically Globalized Store Links

iTunes, Amazon and Microsoft Store links are automatically optimized, making sure every user gets to the right item in their local storefront and you get credit for those sales.

User Choice Landing Page

Let customers choose where to make their purchase. With this "interstitial," your geni.us link becomes a beautifully simple and responsive landing page that you can customize for your audience.

Full Affiliate Program Automation

Add your iTunes, Amazon and Microsoft affiliate IDs once and we'll automatically affiliate each click, earning you more commissions from around the world.

21 - Other Print On Demand Sites

![FanPrint™ logo]

fanprint.com/features?r=4618

How Does It Work?

FanPrint wants YOU to help us make the best fan gear out there!

So how does it work?

Come up a killer slogan or design.

Submit your idea to our curation team by sending through your individual slack channel. Receive a 2.5% designer royals on EVERY sale for that design as well as 40% commission for every shirt sold!

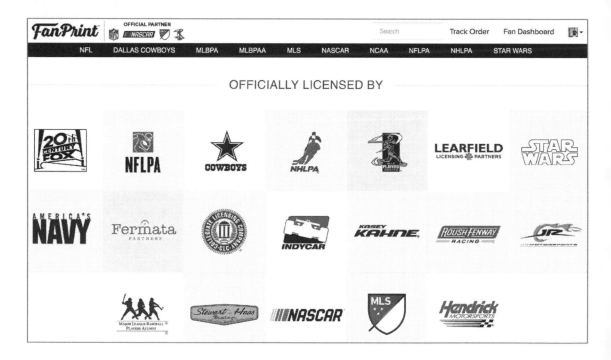

FanPrint has a partnership with Brand Protection Coalition to protect each fan's design on FanPrint.com. If an affiliate/fan sees counterfeit merchandise on social media they can report it here: http://brandprotectioncoalition.com/report

Printful - printful.com

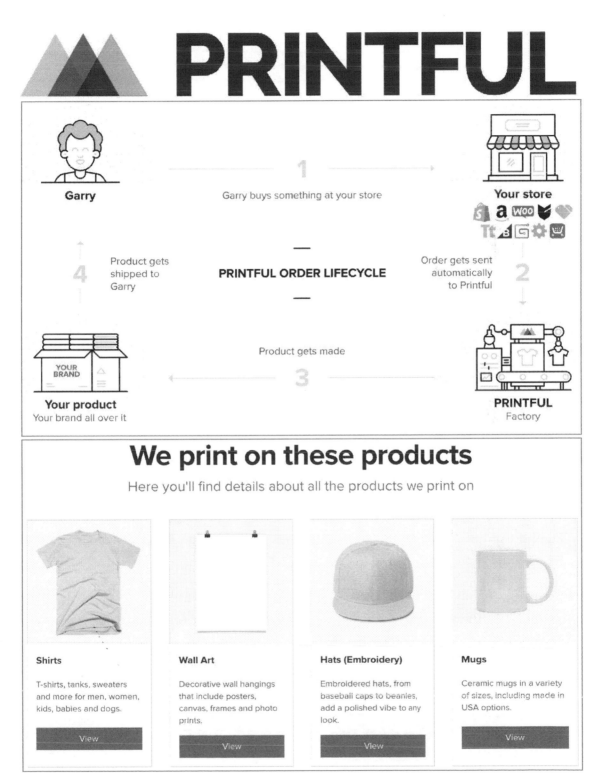

PRINTFUL

Garry

1

Garry buys something at your store

Your store

—

4

Product gets shipped to Garry

PRINTFUL ORDER LIFECYCLE

Order gets sent automatically to Printful

2

—

Product gets made

3

YOUR BRAND

Your product
Your brand all over it

PRINTFUL
Factory

We print on these products

Here you'll find details about all the products we print on

Shirts

T-shirts, tanks, sweaters and more for men, women, kids, babies and dogs.

View

Wall Art

Decorative wall hangings that include posters, canvas, frames and photo prints.

View

Hats (Embroidery)

Embroidered hats, from baseball caps to beanies, add a polished vibe to any look.

View

Mugs

Ceramic mugs in a variety of sizes, including made in USA options.

View

CustomCat - customcat.com

More Than Just T-shirts...
100s of Products

EMBROIDERY | DIGITAL | SUBLIMATION

Get Started Today!

Upload Your Design

Add your design to any product to be printed or embroidered.

Choose Products and Price

Browse products and set prices based on desired profits.

Make Easy Money

Set your goal and details to launch your campaign. Promote your campaign to start generating profit!

CustomInk - customink.com

Custom T-shirts Are Just the Beginning

Customize Hanes Nano-T® T-shirts

Tiny stitches provide comfort and strength.

Make Tie-Dye T-shirts More Fun

Design tie-dye t-shirts for your group.

Polos, Anyone?

Design professional polos that perform.

Products

T-shirts

Athletics

Hoodies &
Sweatshirts

Ladies &
Juniors

Polos

Drinkware &
Koozies

Bags

Hats

Outdoor &
Leisure

Pens &
Supplies

Outerwear

Pants & Shorts

Kitely - kite.ly

Sell *over 250 top quality personalized products* through their worldwide product fulfillment and distribution network across a multitude of sales channels. Their best in market native iOS & Android mobile SDKs, Shopify, and WooCommerce plugins can get you selling in minutes!

Tanks and Vests   from $11.00

Cushions   from $10.00

Mugs   from $4.60

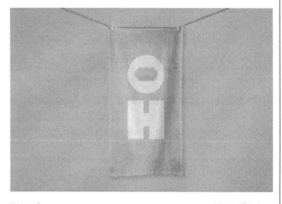

Towels   from $12.00

Snap Cases   from $10.50

Tablet Cases   from $14.97

merchinformer.com/print-demand-sites

viralstyle.com

zazzle.com

cafepress.com

customizedgirl.com

threadless.com

gearbubble.com

sunfrog.com

teespring.com

teepublic.com

society6.com

redbubble.com

spreadshirt.com

22 - Novelty T-Shirt Sites

Need some ideas or inspiration? Unsure of what types of designs sell well?

Then take a look at these novelty/graphic t-shirt sites. Many of them list their best sellers and popular categories so that you can see what other people are buying.

oldglory.com

6dollarshirts.com

bustedtees.com

80stees.com

badideatshirts.com

crazydogtshirts.com

donkeytees.com

246

feelingoodtees.com

headlineshirts.net

T-SHIRT HELL
where all the bad shirts go

tshirthell.com

lookhuman.com

noisebot.com

prankplace.com/

rageon.com

roadkilltshirts.com

248

snorgtees.com

teefury.com

allposters.com

awesome-t-shirts.com

chimpwear.com

computergear.com

davidandgoliathtees.com

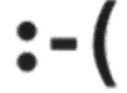

DESPAIR, INC.

despair.com

foulmouthshirts.com

FUNNYSHIRTS.ORG

funnyshirts.org

funnytimes.com

store.glennz.com

lerageshirts.com

thisismerica.com

neatoshop.com

nerdkungfu.com

offworlddesigns.com

BetterThanPants

betterthanpants.com

popuptee.com

supershirtguy.com

teeturtle

teeturtle.com

textualtees.com

trenzshirts.com

whatarethese.net

A COLLECTION OF REALLY COOL TEES & STUFF

whatonearthcatalog.com

23 - Word Clouds

WordArt - wordart.com

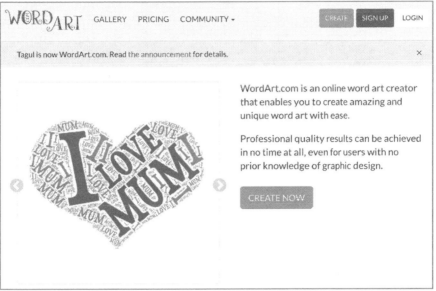

WordItOut - worditout.com/word-cloud/create

JasonDavies - jasondavies.com/wordcloud

Paste your text below!

How the Word Cloud Generator Works

The layout algorithm for positioning words without overlap is available on GitHub under an open source license as d3-cloud. Note that this is the only the layout algorithm and any code for converting text into words and rendering the final output requires additional development.

Go!

Spiral: ◉ Archimedean ○ Rectangular 5 orientations from -60 ° to 60 °

Number of words: 250

Scale: ◉ log n ○ √n ○ n

☐ One word per line

Font: Impact

-90°   0°   90°

Download: SVG

WordClouds - wordclouds.com

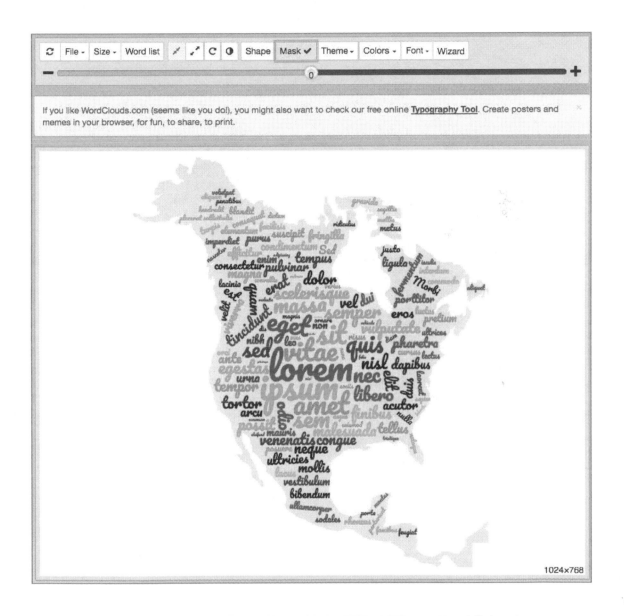

Tagxedo - tagxedo.com

Wordle - wordle.net

Wordle™   Home   Create   Credits   Forum   FAQ   Advanced   Donate

Wordle is a toy for generating "word clouds" from text that you provide. The clouds give greater prominence to words that appear more frequently in the source text. You can tweak your clouds with different fonts, layouts, and color schemes. The images you create with Wordle are yours to use however you like. You can print them out, or save them to your own desktop to use as you wish.

Create your own.

View some examples created by others...

English notebook cover
by Ace Acedemic!

Period G
by Meredith

US Constitution
by Jonathan

Most Common Crossword Answers
by Jonathan

FREE TRIAL of Merch Informer:
MerchInformer.com

Merch Informer

BONUS!
Use code CG15 at signup
to save 15% FOR LIFE!

FREE TRIAL of Make-Merch
Make-Merch.com

$10 REBATE!

Sign up for Make-Merch and then send an email to ThankYouChris@make-merch.com to claim your rebate!

Made in the USA
Middletown, DE
08 January 2019